Awakening
the Sleeping Giant

Maximizing Your Sunday School

Rob Burkhart

Gospel Publishing House
Springfield, Missouri
02-2010

ISBN #0-88243-778-X

Contents

Preface

Awakening the Sleeping Giant: Maximizing Your Sunday School completes a foundational Sunday School training series. This title, together with *Give Them What They Want: Turning Sunday School into a Place People Want to Be* and *Make a Difference! Be a Teacher,* are designed to help teachers revitalize the ministry of Sunday School and to more effectively see students transformed by the Holy Spirit and the Word of God through their efforts.

The premise of this book is that Sunday School plays a pivotal role in the success of the local church and the development of the life of Christians. The author's desire is that teachers and church leaders will embrace a holistic view of Christian education and discipleship. His premise is that when a church is disjointed in its efforts, it will fail to reach its full potential. Teachers and leaders working together to build an intentional infrastructure for ministry will see both spiritual and numeric growth.

In keeping with the direction we have taken with the format of the last two leader's material, we are offering the leader's material that accompanies this volume in an easy-to-store leader's kit. The kit contains a student book, a leader guide, and a compact disk. The compact disk contains downloadable versions of the leader guide in both English and Spanish as well as a PowerPoint presentation designed to facilitate the teaching of the concepts presented in the student book. The leader's kit can be ordered through your Radiant Life supplier.

We are indebted to people in various departments of Gospel Publishing House for the successful completion of this project. Many individuals contributed to the process of producing this text in English and Spanish. Each person's efforts enhanced and further developed this useful resource.

May God use this training tool to multiply the effectiveness of teachers and church leaders.

Introduction

President Franklin Delano Roosevelt declared December 7, 1941, "a day that would live in infamy," for on that day America suffered the greatest defeat in its military history.

But December 7, 1941 was also the day the Japanese Imperial Navy celebrated its greatest naval victory. Meticulously planned, the attack was flawlessly executed. When the Japanese fighter-bombers and torpedo bombers returned to their carrier decks, much of the U.S. Pacific fleet lay at the bottom of Pearl Harbor or had been reduced to piles of burning, twisted metal. Hickham Field, the Scoffield barracks, and other American military installations were reduced to smoldering rubble.

On that bleak day the world seemed destined to be divided and dominated by two great powers. Nazi armies swept across Europe, and the armies of Imperial Japan subjugated Asia and the Pacific. Seemingly nothing could withstand the crushing force of the Axis pincers.

Legend and myth spring from such great events. One such myth is that, following the attack on Pearl Harbor, Admiral

Yamamoto, supreme commander of Japanese naval forces, sent a cable expressing his misgivings. It supposedly read, "I fear all we have done is to awaken a sleeping giant and fill him with a terrible resolve." While the words are not Yamamoto's, they vividly capture the reality of America's war with Japan. America was roused from its isolationist slumber and filled with a terrible resolve to defeat Japan and her Axis allies. Three and a half years later that resolve would be fulfilled in the skies above Hiroshima on the wings of a lone B-29 called the *Enola Gay*.

Before the attack on Pearl Harbor, America sat on the sidelines of the great worldwide conflagration that became World War II. The United States was a second-rate power that lagged far behind the great empires of the day. Regarded as backward and provincial by its friends and disparaged as inferior by its enemies, America watched as the terrible winds of war engulfed the world.

With the attack on Pearl Harbor and the subsequent declarations of war by Hitler's Germany and Mussolini's Italy, America entered the war and became the "arsenal of democracy." Once roused, this sleeping giant became a ferocious adversary to its enemies and a faithful ally to its friends.

World War II ended in Tokyo Bay on the decks of the U.S.S. *Missouri,* an American battleship damaged at Pearl Harbor. Imperial Japan, like Nazi Germany, surrendered unconditionally to the backward and inferior sleeping giant. When the storm clouds finally cleared, the great military might of the Axis powers had been crushed, and their dreams of world domination evaporated into the nightmare of defeat. The great British and French empires lay in ruin and soon disintegrated under the pressure of national independence movements. One by one their former colonies in Africa and Asia sought and won their freedom. And the sleeping giant emerged to lead the free world.

Waking Our "Sleeping Giant"

Sometimes it seems like 1941 all over again.

Our adversary, with dreams of total world domination, has launched a blitzkrieg against the Church. The Church is assaulted from without by a secular society entranced with false spirituality and from within by growing apathy among its members. Many churches reel from the blows of a vicious enemy. Embattled, trapped, and barely hanging on, they struggle against seemingly overwhelming odds.

The Church should be winning. We should be on the offensive, not "hunkered down" praying for mere survival. The gates of hell should be crumbling under our assault, not the other way around.

In all its history, the Church has never had the resources or opportunities this generation possesses. The Church has never been richer, more educated, or better equipped; nor has it faced more open doors. We have great preaching, steadfast prayer warriors, and the power and presence of the Holy Spirit. We live in a time of unprecedented spiritual interest. We have anointed leaders in the pulpit and talented, motivated people in the pews. God has poured out His richest blessings on us. We've never had it better. We should be winning.

Despite great assets and opportunities, many churches are permanently locked in the "slow or no growth" cycle of frustration. Many others are slowly and painfully dying. Their impact on their communities and culture is minimal at best. Vast people groups go unreached. The Church fails to carry out its mission and live up to its potential. Our society hurtles into greater secularism and paganism. More and more people view the Church as a relic of a bygone era.

Long dormant in many churches and abandoned by others is a sleeping giant. It has been disparaged as second-rate and out of step with the needs of today's church. It lacks the flash and dash of newer ways to do ministry. While some church leaders desperately search for new ways to care for their people and reach their communities, this sleeping giant is misunderstood, undervalued, and ignored. In most churches it has been there all along, just waiting for someone to realize its potential and rouse it from its slumber.

What is this "sleeping giant"? Sunday School.

The Church in the Fourth Dimension

The University of Michigan's "Fab Five" were, without a doubt, the most talented five freshmen ever recruited to play Big Ten basketball. They were heralded as the best of the best. Conference championships were inevitable, and Wolverine fans around the country eagerly anticipated a national championship. But although the Fab Five accomplished some incredible things, they never won a national championship.

Despite their talent, great coaching, loyal fans, and the advantages of playing for the University of Michigan and in the Big Ten, the Fab Five never realized their potential. Somehow they weren't able to marshal their talents, focus their energies, and accomplish their most important goals.

Some churches are like that Michigan team. God has given them the gifts and fruit of the Holy Spirit and poured out His blessings. They have great "coaching" in the effective and anointed leadership of a Spirit-filled pastor, but they have failed to realize their potential. What most of these churches need is a comprehensive strategy to marshal the church's resources and focus its energies so it can accomplish its most important goals. Sunday School offers an efficient and effective means to that end.

Understanding the Church in the Fourth Dimension

To fully appreciate the potential of an effective Sunday School in the life of a local congregation, one must first understand the Church. Scripture describes the Church many different ways. A building, a body, and a bride are three of the most powerful analogies. Some understand the Church in the four dimensions articulated in Acts 2:42–47: worship, fellowship, discipleship, and witness. Another way to think about these four dimensions is in terms of a believer's four critical relationships. Believers relate to God in worship, to other believers in community, to themselves in spiritual growth, and to the world in evangelism. Others think about the dimensions of the Church in terms of four priorities: service to God, service to other believers, service to the world, and the spiritual development of believers that energizes and enables all such service.

Defining the Dimensions

An old story tells about five blind men who were asked to describe an elephant. One felt the tail and said an elephant was like a rope. Another felt a leg and said an elephant was like a tree. A third was brought to the side of the elephant and said it was like a wall. After feeling one of the elephant's ears, the fourth blind man said an elephant was like a giant leaf. Feeling the elephant's twisting trunk, the fifth man decided that an elephant must be like a great snake.

All five men were right. Yet all five were wrong. Each had correctly described one part of the elephant, but none had adequately described the whole. Clearly an elephant is more than the sum of its parts.

Trying to describe the Church in terms of its parts is like describing an elephant blindfolded. No description of any one part adequately describes the whole, and the whole is certainly much more than the sum of its parts.

The Church can be described many ways, and each way adds to our understanding of the Church and its mission. Essentially the Church is and does four things. (1) The Church is a worshiping community that gathers to magnify God. (2) The Church is a community of like-minded people connected by their new life in Christ who actively seek to strengthen the bonds of fellowship. (3) The Church is made up of disciples who gather to engage in activities that contribute to their spiritual growth and development. (4) And, the Church is a living witness of Christ on earth and endeavors to proclaim His good news to a lost and dying world through its words and deeds.

Worship

Discrediting this upstart rabbi was the only thing on the Pharisees' minds. Everybody knew nothing good could come from Nazareth. So they asked Him, " 'Teacher, which is the greatest commandment in the Law?' " Jesus replied: " 'Love the Lord your God with all your heart and with all your soul and with all your mind.' This is the first and greatest commandment. And the second is like it: 'Love your neighbor as yourself.' All the Law and the Prophets hang on these two commandments" (Matthew 22:36–40).

Their trap didn't work.

In those few words Jesus summed up all of human history and destiny. From that dark day when Adam and Eve fled the Garden until today and for all the tomorrows until the end of time, there is one great divine imperative: to reconcile sinful humankind to their sinless Creator. At the epicenter of human history is a rocky Judean hill where the tortured, incarnate Son of God announced history's greatest achievement: "It is finished!" The door was opened. The road was cleared. Now nothing stands between God and people except their stubborn refusal to accept God's gracious gift. Salvation and reconciliation await all who repent and believe.

The Church gathers to celebrate new life and to worship its Creator. Through prayer, music, and many other means, the body of Christ expresses its praise and gratitude, exalting the one true God. For many the events of this gathering define worship. But worship must be expressed in the individual lives of believers, in their families, and in their other relationships. Wherever and whenever believers express their love for God, they worship.

There is no one way to worship, no one liturgy, no one style of music, no one way to preach, pray, or praise. Worship practices are shaped by time, place, culture, personality, and preference, and thus they vary widely. These differences are often the source of controversy. They have split churches and have spawned new congregations and even new denominations. Ironically, the differences in the way believers worship the One who prayed that His followers would be one (John 17:22) often result in division and alienation.

While believers may bicker about the details, Christ calls His people to true worship. He says they must worship "in spirit and in truth" (John 4:24). True worship is spiritual. It flows from a dynamic relationship with God characterized by passion and the lifelong pursuit of ever-increasing intimacy with God. True worship is also honest. It flows from the integrity of a life lived to honor God. Any expression of worship that is perfunctory or motivated by a desire to be seen and admired by other worshipers fails that test.

Long ago the prophet Isaiah made clear the distinction between style and substance (Isaiah 1:11–17; 58:1–14). God is not pleased with our worship, no matter the style, if we do not live lives that please Him. Isaiah's warning is stern. Such worship is "meaningless," "detestable," "hated," and a "burden" to God (Isaiah 1:13,14).

Fellowship

Jesus stressed the importance of fellowship when He told His disciples, "By this all men will know that you are my disciples, if you love one another" (John 13:35). He petitioned His Father on His followers' behalf: "May they be brought to complete unity to let the world know that you sent me and have loved them even as you have loved me" (John 17:23). And He taught that the second great commandment—after loving God with one's whole being—is "Love your neighbor as yourself" (Matthew 22:36–40).

Unity is the clear, unequivocal, and often forgotten priority of the Church. God intends for His followers to live out their new life in loving relationships and become the "body of Christ." In 1 Corinthians 12, Paul describes the dimensions of true "body life." The body of Christ, while made up of many different parts, is a single unit (v. 12). Each part of the Body is uniquely gifted to carry out its appropriate function (v. 11), and each is to use his or her gifts to benefit the whole (v. 7). Gifts are not given for private edification or personal exaltation, but to contribute to the healthy functioning of the whole. No part is more or less important than any of the others. All are essential to the Body's health and proper function. All members of the Body should be treated with dignity and honor (vv. 14–18), and all should demonstrate consistent respect, compassion, care, and concern for one another. (See chapter 6 for further discussion on the Church as the body of Christ.)

Loving unity has always been the "gold standard" of the Church. Unfortunately, it has rarely been achieved. Paul's epistles demonstrate how quickly unity was lost and the Early Church fractured into feuding factions. Called by God, Paul became the apostle to the Gentiles. Soon, controversy erupted over whether Gentiles could really become Christians without adopting Jewish customs and practices. That fracture ultimately drew the two great pillars of the Early Church, Peter and Paul, into face-to-face conflict.

Throughout history the organizational unity of the Church has fragmented again and again. The Church was divided between Rome and Constantinople. The Western Church fractured under the weight of Luther's Ninety-five Theses. Soon Calvinists and Anabaptists crowded the field of would-be reformers. Calvin split from Luther, Jacob Arminius rejected Calvin, Henry VIII rejected Rome and established the Church of England—all for the wrong reasons. The Methodists arose out of the Church of England when people responded to the preaching of John Wesley and the music of his brother Charles. Methodism in turn was rejected as new movements grew, including the Free Methodists, the Church of the Nazarene, and others. Then came Azusa Street and the rise of the Pentecostal movement. The Pentecostal movement itself has spawned a dozen or more fellowships (not counting the Charismatics). And that's just one branch of the family tree!

More often than not the Church has failed to be the answer to Christ's prayer for unity. Church fights and splits are legendary. Pastors make jokes about "blessed subtractions" when people leave their congregations in hurt or anger. Denominational leaders quip that a church split is really a church "plant." An oft-repeated (and very sad) little ditty goes like this:

> To live above
> With the saints we love,
> Oh, that will be glory!
> To live below
> With the saints we know,
> That's another story.

Recite this poem in any congregation and watch the heads nod and listen to the "amens" and nervous laughter. But look closer and see the sad reality in the eyes of the victims of church "wars." Despite its many failures, the church is called to be a true community and to foster love, loyalty, and unity among its members.

Inevitably Christians do sometimes disagree with one another.

Differences in time, place, experience, personality, and conscience have led different believers to different conclusions about the Christian life. Such disagreements do not automatically result in a loss of unity. Paul's discussion in 1 Corinthians 8 about meat offered to idols is instructive. He teaches that believers are free to exercise their conscience on a whole range of amoral issues. That's not what's really important. Respect for the sensitivities of other believers is the bottom line. Believers with a "strong" conscience should not flaunt their freedom, and believers with a "weak" conscience should not impose their standards.

Counseling a much younger colleague, a wise old pastor once observed, "The ministry is like a marriage—you have to learn to pick your fights."[1] His point was clear: Some things are worth fighting for, but most things aren't. Spiritual wisdom is knowing the difference. Some things are so essential to the faith that they call us to arms. Other differences are based on personal preferences or one's past, perspectives, or practice and should be tolerated.

Organizational and essential unity are not the same thing. Believers can express their faith through different organizations and bodies of believers and still retain the bonds of Christian unity, but that essential unity must be firmly grounded in the fundamentals of our faith.

Such harmony must be fostered in the church. Unity doesn't just happen; it is the result of efforts to establish an atmosphere of enduring love and loyalty through shared truth, vision, and values.

Truth. The apostle Paul asked in his second letter to the Corinthians, "What do righteousness and wickedness have in common? Or what fellowship can light have with darkness? What does a believer have in common with an unbeliever?" (2 Corinthians 6:14,15) What indeed? While much of the Christian life is left to the individual's conscience, the core truths of the gospel are not. Fundamental doctrinal issues like the inspiration, infallibility, and authority of Scripture; the Trinity; Christ's virgin birth, sinless life,

17

saving work on the Cross, and resurrection; and salvation by grace through faith are not debatable issues. They are the boundaries of unity, for they define what it means to be inside the family of God.

Vision. Shared vision is the cornerstone of Christian service and effective congregational ministry. Believers share a worldview and understanding of life and reality not shared by those outside the fellowship. That common perspective of God, truth, time, eternity, and the meaning of life is an unbreakable bond.

Values. Unity is also the result of shared values. At different times and places believers have valued different things, but the core values of the faith have not changed. These eternal and universal principles may be applied differently, but they are the threads used to weave a unified church. Believers have always agreed that leading a holy life is essential, but they have not always agreed on what it means to lead a holy life. Standards vary widely in different times, places, and cultures. Ultimately, the passion to live a righteous and holy life before God is what unites all believers.

True fellowship is universal. It encompasses believers around the world, across town, across the street, and across the aisle. It supersedes race, language, culture, social and economic status, and the impact of history and tradition. The sign that we are Christians is our love for one another.

Discipleship

Jesus commissioned the Church to "make disciples of all nations, baptizing them . . . and teaching them to obey everything" (Matthew 28:19,20). But what makes true disciples?

True disciples are determined to be like the Master. They understand that discipleship is a lifelong process energized by a continually growing and vital relationship with the Master. Discipleship is the result of an inward transformation that leads to outward manifestations. It is the authentic process of *becoming*, not just "following the rules." Finally, true discipleship is a relational process.

Disciples grow, not only in relationship with the Master, but through relationship with other disciples.

Authentic discipleship impacts five critical areas of life: *knowledge, attitude, action, relationships,* and *the spirit.*

Knowledge. Every disciple is a learner, but not every learner is a disciple. Gaining greater knowledge doesn't automatically result in a changed life. The world is full of biblically literate nonbelievers. The well-known science fiction writer and atheist Isaac Asimov published a two-volume guide to the Bible, but that didn't make him a believer.[2] Receiving biblical and doctrinal instruction is the critical first step for the growing disciple. It is essential but insufficient. Beyond the *facts* of the Scriptures, the disciple must understand biblical *principles.* The Bible is not a rulebook with prescriptions for every circumstance. It is, however, full of principles that, when properly understood, guide believers in every circumstance. These universal principles are equally valuable to all believers at all times and in all places. The circumstances, cultures, and applications vary, but the principles never change.

Beyond learning biblical facts and principles, disciples develop a Christian *worldview,* a way of understanding life and reality that is truly Christian. Believers and nonbelievers see the world very differently. Believers see ultimate truth as something revealed by God, while nonbelievers think truth is discovered. Believers see morality as an absolute standard set by God, while nonbelievers see morality as relative and determined by culture and society. Believers live with the certainty of eternal life, while nonbelievers struggle with the certainty of death. If it seems that believers and nonbelievers perceive and understand the world very differently, it's because they do.

Attitude. Disciples take on the *attitude* of their Master. After his Green Bay Packers came in second two years in a row, Coach Vince Lombardi was determined to make sure it didn't happen again. He papered the locker room with motivational sayings. One came to symbolize the essence of his philosophy, "Winning isn't the most important thing, it's the only thing."[3] In life, attitude isn't the most important thing; it's the only thing. All of life's experiences are mediated through one's attitude. What brings joy to one brings sorrow to another. We can always control attitude.

Consider, for example, the attitude Mary demonstrated in response to the angel's message that she would give birth to the Messiah (Luke 1:38). She knew who she was—God's servant. She knew her life was not her own, and she willingly obeyed.

Action. True disciples will act like their Master. Christians ought to act differently from those in the world around them—not because of some external requirement, but because they are different. Disciples live with a different purpose, perspective, and priorities, and they are enabled by a different power than those in the world. God's love, demonstrated in Christ's sacrifice, should be expressed in the believer's life. "For Christ's love compels us . . . that those who live should no longer live for themselves but for him . . . All this is from God, who reconciled us to himself through Christ and gave us the ministry of reconciliation . . . We are therefore Christ's ambassadors" (2 Corinthians 5:14–20).

Relationships. True disciples relate to others by treating them as the Master would. People relate to others at different levels of intimacy: as strangers, acquaintances, friends, family, and intimates. But Jesus had only one way to treat people. He loved them. He loved the self-righteous Pharisee and the self-indulgent prodigal. He loved His friends and His enemies (Matthew 5:44). He loved those close to Him and those far away. He loved His brothers (1 Peter 2:17), and He loved the world (John 3:16). He loved those who pleased Him and those who broke His heart.

Jesus sees people differently than we do. We see the scars of sin; He sees the image of God. We see their problems; He sees their potential. We see the sin; He sees the sinner as well. We see enemies and adversaries; He sees allies and future friends. We see what has been; He sees what can be. We see the impossible in our lives; He sees the miracles our lives can become. We see the mistakes and failures of the past; He sees the hope and possibility of the future.

Finally, disciples seek in their relationship with other people what God most desires—*reconciliation.* The ministry of reconciliation has been given to the Church (2 Corinthians 5:14–21). Reconciliation to God through Christ is just the first step. People must also come to peace with their past and embrace their future in Christ. Moreover, true reconciliation with God requires reconciliation with others, even those who have offended the most.

The spirit. True discipleship isn't about accepting Christian doctrine, having the right attitude, following a moral code of conduct or treating people decently. It is real spiritual transformation that only comes by grace through faith and is the work of the Holy Spirit in the believer's life to regenerate, sanctify, and empower. It is God at work in the believer.

Nonbelievers can accept Christian doctrine, display a selfless attitude, live righteous, moral lives and treat people with respect and kindness. But those attributes, no matter how laudable, do not make people disciples. The difference isn't on the outside; it's on the inside. The believer is being transformed from the inside out until they no longer "conform . . . to the pattern of this world but (are) transformed" (Romans 12:2) and are "conformed to the likeness of his Son" (Romans 8:29). The true disciple's outward, visible life is a manifestation of an inward, spiritual transformation. It is not a façade that hides our true self. It is an expression of who we really are and what we are becoming in Christ.

Witness

The Church first and foremost bears witness in the world by its *presence.* The very existence of the Church in the world bears witness to the truth of the gospel. For more than two thousand years, dictators and despots have gleefully proclaimed the Church's imminent demise. Yet we're still here. For more than two thousand years, the Church has faced persecution, poverty, and prejudice. Yet we're still here. For more than two thousand years, Christians have been ridiculed, reviled, and rejected by their neighbors, communities, and cultures. We're still here. Churches have been desecrated, confiscated, and destroyed. Their leaders have been threatened, beaten, jailed, and martyred. Believers have been disowned by their families, persecuted by their governments, exiled, and executed. We're still here. Throughout history and in every land, the gospel has been sown with the seeds of sacrifice and watered with the blood of the martyrs. And we're still here.

The very existence of the Church makes an unmistakable proclamation to an unbelieving world that the gospel is true. We are here to stay because our message is true. Unbelievers may not like us. They may see us as dangerous, foolish, or crazy. We may be despised and rejected, but the truth we proclaim cannot be ignored.

The Church's witness in the world begins, not ends, with our existence. The Church not only *is* a witness, it must *bear* witness in the world. The three dimensions by which the Church actively witnesses in the world are *proclamation, people,* and *power.*

The Church bears witness in the world by its *proclamation* of the gospel. Throughout the ages the Church has attempted to accurately communicate the gospel message using every available means—preaching, teaching, music, art, theater, and literature for examples. But perhaps the most powerful forms of proclamation are the daily lives of Christian people, their testimonies, and their simple acts of kindness and generosity.

The Church bears witness in the world by its focus on *people.* The gospel is and always has been about people and their need for the good news of Jesus Christ. Where the Church has truly been the Church, it has rejected the worldly priorities of power, wealth, and prominence, opting instead to meet needs. In rejecting the world's false standards, the Church stands apart from society and reveals the stark contrast between the gospel of Christ and the gospel of conformity to culture. When the Church has lost this focus, it has been at the expense of its moral authority, godly influence, and spiritual power.

The undeniable *power* of the gospel is demonstrated first by the Church's ability to stay the course in the face of opposition. A second way the power of the gospel is proclaimed is in the miraculous interventions of God's Spirit to heal, perform miracles, and answer prayer. Unbelievers may not believe God will hear their own prayers, but they often ask Christians to pray. Jesus warned that a wicked and adulterous generation looks for a sign (Matthew 16:4). Believers today should remember that we live in such a generation. When signs and wonders are a powerful part of the life of the Church, they become an undeniable witness to the gospel.

Getting It Together

The four dimensions of the Church—worship, fellowship, discipleship, and witness—are expressed in many different ways. However they are expressed, they form the bedrock necessary to understand the Church. But how do these pieces become a cohesive whole?

The "Big Rock" Theory

Once a teacher challenged her class with a seemingly unsolvable dilemma. Five objects were placed in front of the class: an empty glass jar, a large rock, gravel, sand, and water. The challenge? Put the rock, gravel, sand, and water in the jar. After several failed attempts by the students, the teacher demonstrated how this task was indeed possible. She explained, "Put the big rock in first, and then add the gravel. The gravel fills in space not taken up by the rock. Then add the sand. It fills in the spaces between the rock and gravel. Finally, add the water. It fills the rest of the space. It's the only way to do it. If you try any other order, it won't work."

Some people try to use the big rock theory to prioritize the four dimensions of the Church. The leaders identify what they believe is most important, thinking that once their "big rock" is in place, everything else will fit. The church name is selected to communicate the essence of their vision, their "big rock," to the congregation and community. For example, evangelism is clearly the "big rock" of churches called "world outreach centers" or use the words *harvest* or *missionary* in their name. For others the "big rock" is worship, evidenced in worship or celebration centers and praise chapels. Still others choose to emphasize fellowship by using words like *family, community,* or *fellowship* in their names.

Underlying the name selection decision is the firm conviction that they are establishing the proper priority for the life and ministry of the church. They believe that if they get this priority right, everything else will fall into its rightful place and the church will be healthy and strong.

There is no agreement as to which of the four dimensions of the church is the real "big rock." At different times and places, churches have chosen to make one or another of these four dimensions their top priority. Various successful church leaders rally support to their point of view, claiming that their way is *the* way to build the church. Their choice of a top priority is based on their personal preferences, perspective, and personality and therefore may not be an appropriate choice for another church.

Yet the influence of larger or more successful churches on leadership's choice of a "big rock" can't be underestimated. Understandably, under different circumstances, the church has needed to emphasize different aspects of its life and ministry. The mistake, however, is believing that an emphasis so valuable to one congregation should be transplanted into another.

This big rock theory doesn't work well in the real world because the other dimensions of the church are ranked in relation to leadership's top priority, causing ministries to be valued (or devalued) according to their influence on this singular vision. Resources (workers, finances, facilities, equipment, and so on) are supplied or withheld from ministries based on their contribution to the central priority. This priority becomes at once the church's primary organizing principle and the standard by which all church life and ministry are measured. Finally, this priority becomes the prism through which the church's life and ministry are viewed. It grants church leaders incredible insight into some areas but simultaneously creates blind spots that hinder them from seeing other critical aspects of church life. Inevitably these other aspects will begin to erode. And those who believe their gifts and callings aren't well suited for the church's key priority will feel as if they are on the outside looking in.

What results is something like the barnyard in George Orwell's *Animal Farm,* where all the animals are equal but the pigs are a little more equal. Church leaders value all the ministries of the church, but their "big rock" is just a little more valuable.

The Corporate Jigsaw Puzzle

Some reject the notion of a big rock. Instead of seeing the church as having a hierarchical structure, they see it as having four equally significant elements. The task of church leadership isn't to prioritize the church's ministries; rather, it is to successfully fit together the many aspects of church life like pieces of a jigsaw puzzle. Leadership's job is to coordinate and balance various ministries. Instead of the challenge being to get the church and all of its ministries to support one key priority, the challenge is to enable the healthy development of all aspects of the church's life and ministry.

In this model the church is thought of as a modern corporation made up of several divisions. Each division has its unique identity and function, and it operates more or less independently of the others. Each division is accountable to leadership and operates under leadership's oversight and guidance. The connections within each division and with its leadership are strong, but the connections between the various divisions are weak.

Just as there are unintended but inevitable consequences with the big rock model, so there are with this approach. For example, ministries engage in *competition.* Since resources are limited, the various ministries must compete for the workers, space, funds, and equipment needed for success. In such an environment, people may come to see fellow church members as competitors and adversaries rather than coworkers and allies. A win for one ministry may be a loss for the others.

This corporate jigsaw puzzle approach can also create *ministry myopia.* People become so focused on their piece that they lose sight of the whole. This institutional blindness to other ministries and to the concerns of others in the church is fertile ground for controversy and injury. Other negative consequences also result, such as missed opportunities for cooperation, unnecessary duplication of programs as ministries expand without regard to other existing ministries, and feelings of isolation and alienation as ministry divisions pursue their agenda with little regard for the "big picture."

Ministry elitism is often another unintended consequence of the corporate jigsaw puzzle approach. People may consider the ministry they are involved in to be the most important, the most prolific, and the most sacrificial, thus making them worthy of more honor and appreciation than others. Those afflicted with ministry elitism fail to appreciate the true value and contribution of others. They turn the biblical admonition to "look not only to your own interests, but also to the interest of others" (Philippians 2:4) inside out and upside down. They want to look to their own interests rather than to the interests of others.

In such an environment, conflict is almost guaranteed. Infighting and political maneuvering become normal parts of church life as people jockey for resources, position, power, and prestige.

Successful leaders are those who can "bring home the bacon" for their ministry, get what they want, and do as they please regardless of the effect on others or even on the church as a whole.

This approach puts a heavy burden on church leaders. No decision pleases everyone, and allocating resources takes the wisdom of Solomon. Leaders are called upon to referee disputes, salve hurt feelings, and bandage bruised egos. Celebrating the accomplishments of one is seen as ignoring and insulting others. Expressing appreciation for one is seen as a lack of appreciation for others. Getting everyone on the same page and headed in the same direction is a monumental task. It's like trying to keep kittens in a box—it requires constant effort and doesn't make anyone (especially the "kittens") happy.

The Right Tool

Both the big rock and the jigsaw puzzle models are widely used. Both have inherent strengths and weaknesses. Both can produce tremendous results, and both can result in tremendous failure. The merits of each can be debated by their respective proponents without any resolution. But that's not the point.

The question isn't whether one of these is better than the other. The question is whether either is the right tool for the job. Is there another more effective and efficient way for the church to marshal its resources, focus its energies, and effectively accomplish what is most important?

For some, finding a truly effective model of local church ministry is like Galahad's search for the Holy Grail—a lifelong, fruitless quest. There is no Holy Grail, no big rock, no magic bullet and no one model of an effective church. However, there are eternal, biblical principles and insights that form the foundation of effective ministry. In the remaining chapters, we'll examine some of these principles and practical ways to implement them in the life of the local church through Sunday School.

Endnotes

[1]Reverend Thomas Skoog, conversation with author, Adrian, Mich., 1984.

[2]Issac Asimov, *Asimov's Guide to the Bible,* 2 volumes, (New York: Doubleday Publishing Company, 1968–1969).

[3]David Maraniss, *When Pride Still Mattered: A Life of Vince Lombardi* (New York: Simon and Schuster, 1999).

The Building Blocks of Effective Ministry

The Christmas Present

It was really, really late one Christmas Eve.

The stockings were stuffed and hung (not by the chimney—they didn't have one—but certainly with care). The house was filled with the sweet aroma of freshly baked holiday treats. The children had been tucked into bed . . . three times . . . and now tossed and turned in anticipation. Brightly wrapped presents were piled under the tree. As the weary father looked around the house, everything seemed ready.

"I think I'll go up to bed. Good night," he called to his wife in the kitchen.

"You forgot, didn't you?" she called back.

"Forgot what?" he asked.

"You have to put Erika's dollhouse together. There won't be time in the morning. It's the one thing she really wanted this Christmas."

He had forgotten. He was in no mood for another late-night

project, but he couldn't stand the thought of disappointing his little girl. So he pulled the box from its hiding place under their bed.

Opening the box, he found a jumble of pieces that made up the walls, floors, ceilings, and roof of the dollhouse. He also found bags of assorted screws, clips, bolts, nuts, washers, and several other things that were obviously important but very mysterious. He had no idea what they were. He pawed through the clutter and found other bags of "easy to assemble" furnishings for the house. Finally, he pulled out the instruction manual that had been buried in the bottom of the box. It looked long enough to contain an original handwritten copy of Tolstoy's *War and Peace.*

The frustrated father was relieved to discover that the manual contained instructions in four languages: Spanish, French, English, and something he took to be Chinese, Japanese, or Korean. He began to read the English version. Two things were quickly obvious. First, whoever wrote the instructions was not a native speaker of English. Second, the writer had never actually assembled one of these houses. The pages were full of diagrams with arrows pointing to "slot a" and "tab b" and recommending this size screw or that kind of clip. (Nowhere did he see anything that explained the mystery pieces.) The "tools needed" list looked like a reorder form from the local hardware store.

It was going to be a long night—a very long night.

"Honey, could I have a cup of coffee?" The whine in his voice was unmistakable.

An hour into the project the fatigued father had assembled, disassembled, and reassembled portions of the house several times. He had too many of some parts and not enough of others, and some parts he couldn't find at all. The mystery parts were still a mystery. Tools, parts, packing material, and instructions were scattered everywhere. The coffee was cold, his wife was in bed, and he was no closer to a completed dollhouse than when he had started. It was then that he noticed something printed on the side of the box lid: "Easily assembled by a child in just 30 minutes!" He thought briefly, but seriously, about getting one of his children up and making them put it together. He thought about putting it all back in the box, wrapping it up, sticking a bow in the middle, and telling his daughter that Grandpa wanted to help her with her dollhouse. (But he liked his dad too much.)

Gradually the dollhouse came together. All the parts really were in the box. There weren't too many or too few. The diligent dad solved the mystery of the mystery parts. "Tab b" really did fit into "slot a." While the "easy to assemble" furniture wasn't all that easy, he finally did put it together and carefully positioned each piece in the proper room.

Triumphantly the father prepared to set the dollhouse, complete with a large red bow taped to the roof, where his daughter would see it when she came down in the morning. He could already hear her squeals of delight. The thought made him smile. But his smile faded when he picked up the dollhouse and found one unused piece. Somehow he had assembled the whole dollhouse without missing it. He had no idea what it was, where it went or how he had been able put the dollhouse together without it. He thought seriously about just throwing it away, but he couldn't. Instead, he set it aside, knowing he would have to disassemble and reassemble the dollhouse one more time—but not tonight.

He went upstairs, climbed into bed, and fell into a deep, exhausted sleep.

Fifteen minutes later his three children were yelling and bouncing on their parents' bed. "Wake up! Wake up! It's Christmas!"

Erika loved the dollhouse.

Introduction

The Church isn't a set of components to be prioritized, processed, and set in order. There is no big rock. The Church isn't a giant jigsaw puzzle made up of pieces that leaders try to fit together. Nor is it a corporation with competing divisions. Moreover, making disciples is more than just another piece of the puzzle.

Another way to think about the Church is as a living organism interacting with the world around it and made up of interdependent and interactive systems. To survive and thrive in a hostile world, the different systems of the church must:

1. contribute to one another;
2. act in concert with one another rather than as competitors;
3. be viewed by church leaders, not as equally important, but as equally essential;
4. act as a single unit, not as independent parts.

The Bible calls the Church a "Body." Each part draws its life and vitality from the whole. Each part enables the proper function of the whole and of the other parts. Each part contributes to the other parts what they need for their proper function. Each part finds its greatest value in being part of the whole. And each part coordinates its functions with the other parts and submits to the will of the whole for the benefit of the whole (Romans 12; 1 Corinthians 12; Ephesians 4:11,12).

Like any body, the Church has systems that must function properly if it is to be healthy and strong. The circulatory system, the endocrine system, the respiratory system, the digestive system, the nervous system, and the skeletal system are all essential. The breakdown of any one of these systems means disaster to all the others. Prioritizing one over another simply isn't possible, for all are inextricably linked.

Suggesting that one part of the church is more important than another or that one ministry can get along without the others is like suggesting that the wings of an airplane are more important than the engines, fuselage, or tail. It's like trying to fly with only the wings or only the engines. Their integration and interrelationship are what make flight possible.

For the church to be healthy, all eight of its systems must function. These systems are the building blocks of the life and ministry of the church. Each must fulfill its role in the Body, for each contributes to the healthy function of the other systems and the Body as a whole. They must exist in a mutually supportive environment in which each is valued, nurtured, and serves and is served by the others. We will look at each of these eight systems in the following pages.

Instruction

The Church teaches. It always has and always will. From the Great Commission to its earliest confessions and catechisms, the Church has viewed teaching as an integral part of its life and ministry. Developing healthy instructional systems is one of the great challenges of the Church and one of its essential tasks.

Three essential components—*content, purpose,* and *methodology* —compose the teaching ministry of the church.

What is the *content* of the church's teaching? First and foremost the church teaches the Bible. Three levels of biblical understanding have already been discussed in chapter 1—*biblical information, biblical principles,* and *biblical worldview.* Biblical information encompasses the characters, stories, history, and doctrines of the Bible. Biblical principles are universal in scope. Regardless of when or where believers live, these principles apply. At this principled level, believers are taught to put their faith to work in daily life. Finally, the church teaches a biblical worldview that encompasses our understanding of life and reality.

A host of other important teachings are built on this foundation. For instance, the church teaches biblical skills for practical living. Believers are meant to live out their faith in every aspect of life. Building a healthy Christian marriage and being an effective parent, child, brother, or sister are all essential skills for Christian living. Dating, courtship, sexuality, and marriage are all aspects of the Christian life that should be addressed in the church's teaching ministry.

The church should also teach practical skills for living the Christian life on the job. It should help believers understand their obligation to employers and other employees. Finding the proper balance between work, faith, and family is critical to living a successful Christian life.

Understanding one's place in the church is another aspect of practical Christian living. Stewardship of time, talent, and treasure should be taught. Christians must understand and act on the truth that all believers are gifted and called for ministry and, as stewards of their gifts, will be held accountable for their service. They must also understand that such practical matters as conflict resolution, their response to authority in the church, and their obligations to their brothers and sisters in Christ are critical to healthy Christian living and the life of the church.

But the Christian faith isn't just lived at home, at work, or in the church. It is lived in relationship to the larger community. What are believers' obligations as citizens? What are their obligations to their neighbors, coworkers, and all of the others they interact with every day, such as mechanics, servers, shop owners, bankers, and other businesspeople? How should believers express their faith in the political arena? Should they serve in the military? The list goes on.

In addition to biblical principles and practical living skills, church identity must be taught. The unique history, doctrines, purposes, and perspectives of one's own congregation and fellowship are an essential part of Christian education. Knowing what makes us "us" is critical to building unity and community. Believers readily admit there are many different and equally valid expressions of the Church in the world. But each church should assert and teach its own heritage or it will inevitably lose its unique identity. Newcomers who don't share the history or tradition must be taught if the values and purposes of the founders are to live on.

The church also must equip believers for ministry in the church and in the community. All believers are gifted and called to ministry. Such gifts must not only be discovered, but also developed and deployed. The church is responsible for enabling the discovery, development, and use of these gifts through its teaching ministry.

Finally, the church teaches service to God and others. Worship is enhanced when believers better understand and appreciate the God they serve. Service to others, as an expression of faith and faithfulness, grows from a better understanding of life in Christ and a growing dynamic relationship with God, other believers, and the larger community.

The *purpose* of instruction is to help believers fulfill God's will in their lives. But what is God's will for believers? In Romans Paul expressed the two sides of God's will. In Romans 12:2 the good, pleasing, and perfect will of God is that believers cease to conform their lives to this world and be renewed and *transformed.* In Romans 8:29 Paul makes it clear that believers are predestined to be *conformed* to the likeness of God's Son. God's will is that believers become like Jesus—not mere imitations, but true reproductions of His character, love, and attitude.

The *methods* the church uses to teach should not only effectively communicate biblical knowledge, principles, and worldview, but also help believers fulfill God's will for their lives. This kind of teaching seeks to engage believers at every level and challenge their emotional lives, behavior, understanding, relationships, and spiritual lives. It uses active learning methods in a highly participatory process.

Evangelism

In response to the Great Commission to go and make disciples of all nations, the Church has always reached out to those who do not know about Christ or have not yet believed.

What must the church do to fulfill Christ's mandate to reach the world? First, it must adequately communicate the need to reach those without Christ. It's not hard to see the need in the desperate, ruined lives of those trapped in the depths of sin. It's not hard to communicate the need of those who live in distant lands, follow strange religions, and engage in practices abhorrent to our culture. Nor is it hard to see the need of the poor, the lost, the addicted, or the cult follower. It is, however, much harder to see the need of the affluent, the well educated, the nice people all around us. But the Bible is clear: There are only two kinds of people in the world, believers and unbelievers. There are only two destinies, heaven and hell. There are only two paths, and one leads to heaven and the other to eternal punishment. There is only one door into God's presence and only One who brings eternal life—Jesus.

The hallmarks of such a church are *vision, passion, courage, sacrifice,* and *skill.*

Believers' *vision* is critical to their witness. How should believers view those who have not yet found Christ? Some look at nonbelievers' sterling character or lofty principles and see no need. Others look at their sin and see no hope. But the effective witness sees both their need and the hope that springs from God's gracious hand.

Believers must be *passionate* in their love for God and have compassion for the lost. Only the love of God and love for God can truly motivate believers to reach their world.

Evangelism demands *courage* and *sacrifice.* Being a faithful witness means having courage to speak when persecution and suffering may result. Willing sacrifice is the second trait of a faithful witness. Sharing one's faith always has a cost. Therefore, believers must be brave.

But passion and courage are enhanced when coupled with *skill.* Believers who truly understand their faith, articulate it clearly, and speak from the wellspring of their own lives and experiences are the most powerful witnesses. Such believers know that everything about their lives is their witness and not just their words. Thus, they develop a truly Christian lifestyle in which their walk is consistent with their talk.

Finally, such believers understand that evangelism is a process and not just a product. They willingly develop long-term relationships with nonbelievers. They understand that evangelism is, in a sense, preconversion discipling and are willing to take on the task. They know that the "not yet believer" will be drawn to Christ by their interaction and positive experiences and that the journey to faith may take a very long time.

Assimilation

New believers or newcomers must not only be reached and touched, but also welcomed into the church family. If a church doesn't become "their church," they ultimately and inevitably drift away. Assimilation is an intentional process that begins with a *personal touch* of welcome and acceptance. Newcomers need to know others and be known so they can develop positive relationships. This happens only through face-to-face interaction. Furthermore, assimilation requires *finding a place* in the Body. Feeling needed and included is the next critical step in the process. And finally, these new believers must be *provided for.* The church takes care of its own. Being part of God's family means that the church and its people willingly provide care, support, and help as needed. If the church fails to reach out and meet real needs, newcomers have every right to conclude that, despite all the rhetoric, they really don't belong.

Effective assimilation requires several practical steps. Someone must make the newcomers' smooth transition into the Body their personal concern. Every believer should be concerned about those new in the faith, but sometimes everybody's business is really nobody's business. Assimilation also requires keeping good records. Without contact and other critical information, assimilation will be haphazard at best. Assimilation takes time and consistent effort. Helping newcomers find a meaningful task or role in the church is another important step.

Care

The first crisis the apostles faced after the Day of Pentecost wasn't external persecution but internal dissension. Two events threatened the very existence of the fledgling church. The first was a crisis of character in the persons of Ananias and Sapphira (Acts 5). The second was a crisis of care (Acts 6). A dispute, complete with overtones of racial discrimination, arose over the distribution of help and support for widows. Clearly the church always has been a place where the needs and concerns of its members matter.

Need-meeting ministry is one of the hallmarks of an effective church. People have a variety of physical, social, emotional, and spiritual needs. The church should help meet physical needs, but its care should not end there. People need to feel valued and important. They need to be noticed, welcomed, accepted, and included. They need to be involved in meaningful ministry and find fulfillment and purpose in their lives. They need the love, compassion, and support of a family of like-minded people who truly care.

The church's care for its own and for the community is most clearly demonstrated in times of crisis. Illness, financial need, or other personal crises are opportunities for the church and its people to show that they really do care. Believers should remember that "the least of these" whom Jesus taught us to serve were the hungry, the naked, the sick, and the imprisoned. The poor and desperate hear the gospel gladly.

Caring in the church must take place on two levels. First, individual believers are obligated to do all they can to meet the needs of which they are aware. Second, the church must show organized, corporate caring as we saw in the apostles' organized distribution of aid to needy widows. They established a procedure, designated responsible leadership, and gathered the needed resources. They developed a plan to care and cared enough to act on their plan.

In short, people don't care how much we know until they know how much we care.

Community

The church should be a true community, a great big extended family in which the bonds of love and loyalty are cemented by the power of grace. The development of true community is an extension of the process that begins with conversion and assimilation. Five critical components—*identity, inclusion, involvement, importance,* and *indivisibility*—mark the family.

Being family is ultimately about a shared *identity.* Families share heritage, history, love, purpose, perspective, and pride. Ultimately, family identity is the source of a person's self-definition. It is the way we understand ourselves, our lives, our purpose, and others. It means that we have been chosen by and that we have chosen this group of people. Second, family means being *included* in the lives of others and the life of the family. No longer on the outside looking in, family members have a "place at the table." Joining the family is a subtle shift between "them" and "us." Family also means being *involved,* having something important to do that cements our place in the family and contributes to its life and health. Fourth, family means being an *important* and valued member of the community. Everyone matters. And finally, family means being *indivisible.* The bonds of true family are never really broken. Disputes, disappointments, and even disillusionment may come, but the cords of grace and love and loyalty can never really be broken.

True unity and community don't just happen. They are created by an act of the will and sustained by a lot of hard work. Building the family of God requires wisdom, not wishful thinking. It demands self-sacrifice, not self-interest.

Spiritual Life and Vitality

The fundamental reality of the gospel is vital spiritual life and transformation by the power and presence of God through the work of His Holy Spirit. Without true spiritual life, worship is just liturgy and Christian education is just religious instruction. If conversion ceases to be a miraculous encounter in which believers pass from death to life, it's just mental assent to human creeds. Christian service and ministry devolve into charity and good works. Prayer becomes just another religious exercise practiced for its personal benefits but devoid of any real power.

Spiritual life isn't so much taught as it is caught. It comes from a direct and personal encounter with the living God. Knowing about God and knowing God are not the same thing. As believers open their lives to the Holy Spirit through repentance, prayer, worship, and the study of God's Word, they experience the powerful transforming presence of God. We were created for vital spiritual communion with God. This was lost in Eden, and is what Christ died to restore.

But spiritual life and vitality fade if not renewed. Fresh from his encounter with God, Moses visibly radiated God's presence. He literally glowed. To keep from terrifying his people, Moses put on a veil. Each time he met God, Moses took off the veil and glowed again. But behind the veil the glory faded (Exodus 34:29–35; 2 Corinthians 3:12–18). Paul records an interesting detail: Even when the glory faded, Moses wore the veil. The inward glory was gone, and the outward covering remained.

A divine encounter inevitably leads to outward changes. But the sad history of the Church and many Christians is that long after the reality of their encounter with God has faded, they maintain the outward trappings. These external manifestations of spiritual life harden into pharisaical, legalistic rules devoid of real spiritual life. They become the dead letter of the law.

Continual renewal of the power and presence of the Holy Spirit in the believer's life is essential for healthy Christian living. Anointed worship experiences are part of the answer. But the believer must also develop the disciplines of the spiritual life, including fasting, prayer, and regular study of God's Word. The value of others encouraging, challenging, and supporting the pursuit of spiritual vitality can't be overlooked or overestimated. Spiritual vitality is an individual challenge best met in the context of a caring body of believers.

Christian Action

The Church is, always has been, and always should be an aggressive force transforming the world. God intended it to be so in His determination to bring reconciliation to the lost and dying world He loves so much. That fact brought the wrath of history's despots, dictators, and demagogues down on the Church, for they rightly understood that the Church and its message were dangerous to their dreams of domination.

The Church has historically responded to culture in three very different ways, which can be demonstrated in the life and ministry of Moses. During Moses' first forty years, he was *absorbed* into Egyptian culture. He was no different than any Egyptian of the time. Some churches and believers have been absorbed into their culture and are indistinguishable and invisible. Rather than transforming their world, they have been transformed by their world. But this isn't God's plan for the Church or the believer.

During the second forty years of Moses' life, he *rejected* Egyptian culture. He herded Jethro's sheep on the back side of the desert. Throughout the centuries some believers have determined that the proper response to the world is to withdraw. Stylites built towers and monks built monasteries. Many today reject the world around them by withdrawing into the life and fellowship of their church. They do all they can to separate themselves from the world. They take Paul's admonition to the Corinthians to "come out from them and be separate" (2 Corinthians 6:17) literally and to an extreme. These do not transform the world. They view the world and the world views them as strange, alien, and incomprehensible. Each ignores the other, and they follow separate paths. But hiding from the world isn't God's plan either.

During the last phase of Moses' life, he returned to Egypt and *interacted* with the culture. He brought God's Word, proclaimed God's will, did God's work, and demonstrated God's miracle-working might. He engaged the culture, and it was forever transformed.

The Church must not surrender to the world and it must not run away and hide. On the contrary, the Church should declare God's Word, carry out His will, do His work, and depend on His miracle-working power. The Church should act like the Church, preaching good news to the poor, proclaiming freedom for the prisoners and recovery of sight to the blind, releasing the oppressed, and proclaiming the year of the Lord's favor (Luke 4:18,19).

The Church exists to make a difference, not just be different.

Equipping for Ministry

Ministry is a magnificent burden. It is at once the most over-whelming obligation and the greatest privilege believers can have. God miraculously gifts His children so they can partner with Him to fulfill His eternal purposes in the world. There is no higher call-ing or greater honor than serving God, His Church, His people, and His purposes in the world. Yet as stewards of their gifts, the recipients are held accountable for their use (1 Peter 4:10). Thus, there can be no greater burden and no greater obligation than to employ one's gifts, talents, and life in the cause of Christ.

"Every-member" ministry is the goal of the Church. While not all believers are called to vocational ministry, all are indeed called to minister. Every believer has an important function to fulfill in the body of Christ. When God calls, God enables. He distributes the gifts of the Spirit to His followers to supernaturally enable their service. While the gifts and ministry differ, believers are to use their gifts in harmony with one another under the lordship of Christ. God gifts the Body with all it needs for robust health and redemptive ministry.

Tragically, most believers think ministry is reserved for someone else. Most don't believe they are called or gifted. They think they have nothing to offer the Body. Most do not know their calling and cannot identify a specific place of ministry. Many are too busy, too preoccupied with work, family, and friends to invest time and energy in fulfilling God's call to ministry. Most do not function in ways that meet needs or contribute to the Body. The result is a crippled church struggling to fulfill its great mission.

Why? Some believers are unaware of their calling and gifts. Others view ministry as something the church hires the pastor to do. Still others are the victims of burnout; overworked and underappreciated in the past, they refuse to be trapped again. But many others have simply never had the opportunity to develop their gifts and callings because church leaders have made no consistent or conscientious effort to equip them for ministry.

Some church leaders lack the skills to teach and train. Others are afraid of trained and involved laity. They worry that they will lose their place if laypeople are equipped to serve. Some are afflicted with perfectionism and can't trust anyone else. Some just don't understand their role as one who equips others for service (Ephesians 4:11,12). The reasons are many and varied, but the result is always the same: failure.

When church leaders invest in their people and help them develop their gifts and callings, great things happen. Strength (Ephesians 4:12), unity (4:13), maturity (4:13), stability (4:14),

43

development and growth (4:15), and health (4:16) all flow from a people equipped for service and engaged in ministry.

Equipping for ministry is the proper responsibility of apostles, prophets, evangelists, pastors, and teachers (Ephesians 4:11,12), but they are not ultimately responsible for what believers do or don't do with their gifts. Each believer is responsible to respond to God's call and use his or her gifts in His service. Leadership is responsible, however, to proclaim the truth of God's call, provide opportunities for others to develop their gifts, invest in others, and help believers invest their lives in meaningful ministry.

The lack of called, gifted, and equipped men and women who willingly take their place in the ministry and serve with joy and excellence is the church's greatest handicap. It is also proof of leadership's greatest failure.

The Capstone

The capstone is an architectural marvel, and it is the most critical element in an arch. To build an arch, stones were stacked vertically on either side of the opening. A framework was built to support the stones that curved upward and inward to form the arch. At the top of the arch, a skillfully crafted, wedge-shaped capstone was carefully set in place. If all went as planned, the weight of the capstone would create enough pressure on the stones underneath to hold them together and in place. The supporting framework was then removed. What had been a pile of stones was transformed into an arch capable of supporting great weight.[1] Such arches have stood for centuries without mortar, steel reinforcement, or anything else to hold them together except gravity and the capstone.

Church leaders readily acknowledge the importance of the building blocks of effective ministry. Some prioritize them. Others try to make them fit together like a jigsaw puzzle. But in the final analysis, what is needed is a capstone. Something needs to be in place to hold the pieces together and make it possible for them to function as a single, solid structure. Sunday School can be that capstone. Let's take a second look at each of these critical elements.

Instruction

Sunday School is a place of instruction. As an age-graded, small-group experience, the Sunday School is ideally suited to teach believers in ways appropriate to their physical, emotional, social, and spiritual development. When teachers are properly trained and provided with appropriate curricula, facilities, equipment, and other needed resources, and when appropriate teacher-learner ratios are observed and methodologies that encourage active learning are employed, Sunday School is an effective learning environment. But too often Sunday School is a great idea badly done.

Evangelism

The Sunday School can be a highly effective and integrated evangelism and assimilation strategy. It is a perfect place to communicate passion for the lost and equip believers with the skills needed to effectively communicate the gospel. It is a place where believers can pray together for unsaved loved ones and for one another.

The Sunday School class is an ideal place to introduce seekers to the gospel and to the church. Many who would never come to a worship service would come to Sunday School classes that meet real-life needs. Others will come to special events sponsored by the Sunday School. Parents, even those who are not yet believers, want their children to have a religious and moral education. Still others will come to be with friends or family.

Through the Sunday School, teachers can develop and maintain records that allow the church to stay in touch with nonbelievers and reach out to them. Class members can develop friendships inside and outside the class that help lead nonbelievers to Christ.

Finally, the church has a ready-made army of "evangelists."

Sunday School teachers, workers, and students can be trained and deployed. Using the Sunday School as a strategic base to follow up on nonbelievers and reach them is a natural extension of its mission and organization.

Assimilation, Care, and Community

Sunday School has the elements needed to effectively assimilate newcomers, provide ministry and care, and build unity and community. Because the Sunday School is an age-graded, small-group ministry, new people find a welcoming environment. They are far more likely to meet someone of similar age, interest, or experience and form a friendship. People may attend worship regularly and remain an anonymous face in the crowd, never belonging. As a small group, the Sunday School class is better able to notice someone missing or in need, to care, and to do something to meet needs.

Because the Sunday School collects and keeps contact information and attendance records, newcomers and old-timers are less likely to slip through the cracks and out the back door. Following up on newcomers and absent members is a critical part of the Sunday School's ministry. But Sunday School must also equip others and engage them in this vital ministry. The goal is to develop a body of believers aware of the newcomers in their midst and sensitive to the needs, hurts, and concerns of old friends.

Sunday School is the place to build unity and identity. By consistently communicating the church's history, doctrine, and perspectives, the Sunday School creates a shared understanding and a shared sense of vision and purpose.

Spiritual Life and Vitality

Sunday School is the ideal environment for developing and maintaining spiritual vitality. It's a place where believers can discover more about God. It can be a laboratory of the Holy Spirit in which people experience the power and presence of the Holy Spirit as they pray, learn, and grow together. Learners can develop trusting friendships in Sunday School with those whom they can share their spiritual triumphs and trials. These friends are much more likely to notice when another believer struggles and to reach out with loving concern.

Christian Action

Sunday School class is an ideal setting for informing, motivating, organizing, and carrying out ministry in the world. As class members apply their faith in practical ways, they explore biblical teaching, reflect on their own faith walk, and are stretched and challenged to grow.

Sunday School classes can take on an almost limitless array of ministries, ranging from issues of social justice to the individual needs of hurting people. A Sunday School class could support the ministry of a crisis pregnancy center, help build a Habitat for Humanity house, establish a food pantry, visit prisoners or nursing home residents, or get involved with neighborhood public schools and provide after-school activities and tutoring for struggling students. The list is as long as the need.

Equipping for Ministry

Finally, Sunday School offers an ideal format for ministry training. Classes dealing with specific ministry skills can be offered in addition to or as part of existing classes. Evangelism, teaching, altar ministry, ushering and greeting, secretarial support, and other ministries within the church could be taught in Sunday School.

Sunday School also offers tremendous opportunities for mentoring and on-the-job training. Believers can gain the practical skills of service while working with those already involved. These transferable skills ultimately benefit other ministries of the church.

People can be found faithful in little before they are given much. Such involvement brings them into contact with more experienced teachers and workers who can mentor and support their development.

Last Thoughts

Church leaders have long recognized the value of these building blocks of ministry. What has been missing in many churches is a way to bring them together and organize them for maximum impact. Because Sunday School has been viewed only as a vehicle for instruction, its potential in these other areas has been overlooked. Many church leaders have not expected, organized, or equipped the Sunday School to meet those needs.

Endnotes

[1] *World Book Encyclopedia,* 1957 ed., s.v. "arch."

The Sunday School and the Local Church

The Parable of the Problem Deacon

Once there was a pastor who loved God, loved his people, and loved to worship. Each Sunday he led his congregation in exciting, Spirit-filled, anointed worship and preached outstanding sermons. Members of his congregation appreciated his ministry and thought their church was the best. Even the townspeople thought they were really fortunate to have such a fine pastor and wonderful church in their community.

On a bright spring day, one of his deacons came to visit.

"Pastor," he said, "you know how much we love and appreciate you and your ministry. You really are the best. The worship services and your preaching are great. But there's a problem."

"A problem?" asked the pastor. The pastor was surprised. You see, this deacon (unlike some others the pastor had known) was always supportive and positive.

"Yes, Pastor. We have a problem. Our worship services are always outstanding and your preaching is great. But we never really get to know one another. Some feel like our church is just a gathering of strangers and not a real family of brothers and sisters. I was wondering if maybe we could get people together in smaller groups so they could get to know each other better. Then they might feel more like a real family."

The pastor, being a wise and sensitive man, realized the deacon was right and listened to his advice. That's how the church came to organize small groups. It was very good.

Then on a sultry summer afternoon that made the pastor glad the church had invested in air conditioning, the deacon paid a second visit.

"Pastor," he said, "our worship services are better than ever. Those new fellowship groups are great. People are really starting to feel like a family. I think that helps us worship better, don't you? But . . ." (The deacon paused for a long time and stared at his shoes.)

Oh boy, here it comes, thought the pastor. "But . . . what?" he said.

"Well, Pastor, I hate to bring it up, but we've got another problem. You see, people really enjoy getting together, but sometimes they want to be with people their own age. Adults like a chance to be with other adults without their children around. Kids get bored with all the adult talk and want to be with other kids. And the teenagers—well, you know how they are. So I was wondering if you thought it would be a good idea to organize different groups for different ages. They could meet at the same time and even in the same place. We could ask some of the adults to lead groups for the kids. I think it would help, don't you?"

The pastor, who had two teenage children himself, understood completely. So that's how it happened that leaders were selected and groups for children, teens, and adults began meeting. And it was very good.

The leaves were golden and a hint of the winter to come was in the air when the deacon paid a third visit to his pastor.

"Pastor," he said, "worship is great, and these new groups are going great. You really had a good idea. But . . ." (Again the deacon paused to inspect his shoes. It was becoming a habit.)

"There's another problem?" interrupted the pastor.

"Well, yes. How did you know?"

"Just a guess. What is it this time?"

"When we get together, people want to talk about our faith. Sometimes they have questions we can't answer, and some people say things that aren't right. And the children, Pastor, don't know much at all. Now don't get me wrong. Your sermons are tremendous. But maybe it would be good to teach people how to study the Bible and have teachers who can explain the Bible and answer questions. We could take some time in our groups to study the Bible. A lot of our group leaders would make great teachers."

It was the pastor's turn for a long pause. (He realized his shoes could use a good polishing.) He thought long and hard but knew that he could never teach everything his people needed to know in his preaching. So that's how it happened that teachers were recruited and trained and study material selected. The groups began to study God's Word as well as get to know one another and develop real friendships. And it was very good.

On the deacon's fourth visit, snowflakes were falling gently. His pastor met him at the door, took his coat, invited him into his office, and offered him a cup of hot chocolate. He looked at the deacon across the desk and wondered what it was this time.

"Pastor," began the deacon, "you're probably wondering why I'm here."

"Not really," said the pastor.

"Well, everything is going so well I almost hate to bring it up."

"But that's not going to stop you, is it?"

"I'm afraid not, Pastor. You see, sometimes people miss their group meetings. They are sick or have some other problem. People have been hurt and haven't come back. Worst of all, sometimes people are struggling in their walk with the Lord and stay away. People in the group don't always check up on those who are missing. Then they feel like we don't care about them."

"That's terrible," interrupted the pastor.

"Wait Pastor, that's not all. Sometimes new people visit our groups. Some of them aren't even believers. Our people feel awkward and don't always know what to say or how to make them feel comfortable. Then they don't feel welcome and don't come back. Some of the visitors get offended. People have stopped bringing their friends because they feel they aren't treated well when they get there. It's a real problem."

"I can see that," said the pastor. "But I'm sure you have a suggestion."

The deacon was a little taken aback by his pastor's tone but took a deep breath and plowed ahead.

"I was thinking, Pastor, that we should keep a list of all the people in each group. You know—get their names, addresses, e-mail addresses, and phone numbers. Then we could do a better job of taking care of them. If we could get that information from new people, we could give them a call and let them know we were glad they came. I know there are people in the groups who would love to help out this way. But we didn't want to go ahead without talking to you about it."

And that's how it happened that records were created. Group leaders asked some members to help make sure that missing members were contacted and new people were welcomed. The groups began to really care about one another and help out when people were sick or had problems. New people appreciated the interest and concern of group members and came back week after week. Soon many of them were coming to church on Sunday. People who weren't believers came to Christ as group members shared their faith. It was very good.

The next time the deacon came to visit, the pastor looked out his office window and saw him pull into the parking lot. The deacon's umbrella opened, and he jogged across the parking lot dodging puddles. The pastor thought about leaving—he did have hospital calls to make. He thought better of it but did slip into the sanctuary to pray for patience.

Ushered into his pastor's office, the deacon waited nervously.

"You're not here to tell me we have another problem, are you?"

"I'm afraid so, Pastor. You see, the groups are growing, and we are running out of space. A lot of people are facing scheduling conflicts—work and school schedules and all that. Getting equipment and supplies to make our group meetings the very best has also been a problem. The finance committee is starting to get a little concerned. It's not really good stewardship."

"Are you saying we should stop having these groups?"

"Oh no, Pastor. I think that would be a mistake. We were just thinking we could make some changes that would make it better."

"Well, what changes did you have in mind?"

"Some of us were thinking that we could move the groups to the church. We have plenty of space, and it would be a lot more convenient. Maybe we could all meet at the same time."

"Okay. I can see that meeting at the church would be a lot more convenient. But when were you thinking of doing this?"

"Well, believe it or not, Pastor, we were thinking of Sunday morning an hour or so before worship. There are few scheduling problems on Sunday, and people are going to be here anyway. It makes a lot more sense than another night out."

The pastor leaned back in his chair and contemplated the ceiling. (It seemed like forever to the deacon, who wondered what the pastor was looking at all that time.)

Finally, the pastor answered. "I like it. Let's do it. Do you think we should give it a name? Then people will know that they are coming to a Bible study group where they can fellowship with people their own age . . . a group that will welcome them and care about who they are . . . a group where they belong . . . a group that will reach out to new people and help them find Christ and become part of our fellowship . . . a group that will help them grow in their relationship with the Lord and become more like Jesus . . . a group that will help them apply the truths of the Bible to everyday life . . . a group that will help them learn to minister and serve others."

"A name?" pondered the deacon. Now it was his turn to contemplate the ceiling. "I don't know, Pastor. What do you think?"

"Well, how about calling it 'Sunday School'? 'Sunday,' because that's when we meet, and 'School,' because that's where we can learn to be like Jesus."

"Sunday School?" The deacon repeated it as if he were trying to get used to it. "It's a strange name, but I think I like it," said the grinning deacon.

And it was good—very, very good.

Introduction: The Great Form and Function Debate

When it comes to Christian education, many church leaders are involved in a great "form and function" debate. They embrace the functions of Christian education and disciple-making in the church but reject as passé and obsolete the form of Sunday School. They see it as an old tool no longer suitable for today's church and society.

Two different approaches result from this rejection. Some abandon the Sunday School as a quaint anachronism and attempt to create other forms to carry out the same function. Another response is to view the Sunday School as worthwhile but insufficient. They develop other "niche" ministries to fill the gap that Sunday School supposedly leaves. Churches ultimately develop a menu of ministries to meet a variety of needs. These new specialized ministries are narrowly targeted and demand a significant investment of time, talent, and other resources.

Both of these approaches create concerns. New ministries are almost always untested and lack a proven track record. There is no guarantee that an idea that worked in one place will work in another. Nor is there any proof that a ministry designed to meet a need in one context will be as successful in another. A church can jump from one ministry fad to another. New ministries often lack the curricular and training support essential for success. It takes much more than a good idea to make a ministry successful.

The multiplication of these new forms creates a tremendous demand for people, finances, space, equipment, and the other tools needed for success. Very often church resources are stretched to the breaking point. While providing a wide variety of ministries, the church may not do any of them very well. They have quantity but not quality. Leadership must invest time in researching, developing, and maintaining these ministries. This time and energy might be better spent elsewhere.

The motivation to replace Sunday School or augment it with niche ministries is often a result of Sunday School's failure to produce the desired results. The logic is simple and direct. Leaders take stock of their Sunday School and quite rightly decide that it is failing and should be replaced with something more effective or be augmented with other ministries. They reason that Sunday School is failing because it is an out-of-date or flawed form of Christian education that no longer meets the need.

Before drawing any conclusions as to whether Sunday School is viable for disciple-making in the local church, several things should be noted.

There can be no "function" without a "form." Nothing gets done without a way to do it. The church cannot make disciples without a way to disciple. It cannot reach a lost and dying world without a way to evangelize. The church cannot accomplish anything without the mundane and ordinary elements of a "form": *strategy, organization, implementation,* and *evaluation.*

If an organization abandons a form, it risks losing the function. If the function is no longer needed, then losing the form doesn't matter. For example, when people replaced horses with cars, cities replaced hitching posts with parking meters. But if the function is valued and the form is abandoned, then another form must be created and implemented or the function itself will be lost. Leaders always hope a new form will improve the function. The risk is that the new form may end up worse than the old. That happened when Coca-Cola introduced a new form of its product only to discover that people really liked "old Coke" better than "new Coke."

The function of disciple-making is essential to the life and ministry of the church. To some Sunday School is like a hitching post, something past its usefulness. But the new forms may not be any better. In fact, they may be worse. The church that abandons Sunday School may end up worsening their discipling process rather than improving it.

A dynamic relationship exists between form and function. When created, a form is designed to carry out a certain function. Function defines form. But once created, a form then determines function. A tool may be designed to do a certain job, but it is the quality of the design that determines how well it ultimately does the job. Both a quartz watch and a sundial are designed to tell time. One just does it much better than the other.

Forms must be constantly refined and improved. The design, use, and redesign of a form is the continuing process of improving quality and performance. A design that allows this kind of adaptation is ultimately more useful than one that does not. Designs that have been around for a while are often better than new designs, because the "bugs" have been worked out.

Sunday School has been designed, field-tested, refined, and redesigned for more than two hundred years in various settings. That long experience brings a quality that new and innovative forms cannot possibly possess; they just haven't been around long enough or used in a wide variety of settings.

Really useful forms must be both effective and efficient. They must be effective in that they meet the need. Snow skis are great on the slopes but not on the water. They are efficient in that they carry out the function well. A form may be effective in that it does the right thing but not be efficient. It's the wrong tool for the job. On the other hand, a form may be ineffective in that it doesn't meet the need but efficient in that it does what it does well. The ideal is a form that is both highly effective and efficient. Throughout its history, the Sunday School has proven that it is both an effective and efficient tool in the disciple-making process.

Another factor in the form and function debate is the user. A well-designed tool in unskilled hands cannot perform to its full potential. A poorly designed tool in the hands of a skilled artisan can perform well beyond its design. The virtuoso violinist can make any old beat-up fiddle sing. But a Stradivarius in the hands of an amateur is just another violin.

Many churches are "fiddling" around with Sunday School and not exploring its full potential. No serious attempt is being made to invest resources, recruit and train workers, build the organization, or do the hard work it takes to build a successful ministry. Sunday School is not out-of-date; it is just "out of steam," and no one is stoking the boiler.

Some designs are so specific that they aren't much good for anything else. *Some designs are more flexible and adaptable than others.* They can be effectively used in many different settings and ways. The Sunday School design is an effective and efficient instructional system, but inherent in its design is the capacity to carry out other functions critical to the life of the church. That carrying capacity includes building connections and caring systems, assimilating newcomers, training workers, and developing healthy bonds of love in the Body. These are the natural "byproducts" of the design and the effective implementation of a quality Sunday School.

A form also must interact well with its environment. A perfectly good tool is worthless if it is designed for one environment and can't adapt to another. It is just as worthless if it doesn't "fit" with the other elements in its environment or cannot meet the needs and demands that confront it.

On April 4, 1943 an American B-24 named "Lady Be Good" disappeared after taking off from its base in Soluch, Libya to fly north across the Mediterranean and bomb the harbor at Naples, Italy. No evidence of the plane or her crew was found for sixteen years until her wreckage was discovered . . . 440 miles south of Soluch, deep in the desert. When the wreckage was examined, it was discovered that the crew had bailed out taking their "Mae West" life preservers with them.[1] What was effective and essential to survive in water was useless in the desert.

Some forms of ministry are ill suited to their environment. They don't fit; they can't adapt. They cannot do for the church what it truly needs.

Finally, an effective form has staying power. Effective designs are based on sound principles and get the fundamentals right. There are hundreds (perhaps thousands) of different kinds of knives. But the basic design is the same. Each has been adapted to a specific function, but all share the same fundamentals—a blade, a cutting edge(s), and a handle or grip. That basic design hasn't changed in thousands of years. The Sunday School has great fundamentals and operates on solid educational and spiritual principles. That's why it has been around so long.

Choosing a Form

Is the Sunday School still an effective and efficient way for the church to carry out its important disciple-making responsibilities?

The best way to answer that question is to look at form and function. What is a disciple-making ministry supposed to do? Can the Sunday School do that well?

One way to think about the disciple-making function is to look again at the four essential components of the church (see chapter 1) and ask some pointed questions.

Can the Sunday School contribute to worship?
Can the Sunday School help build a sense of community?
Can the Sunday School enable the healthy spiritual development of believers?
Can the Sunday School reach the lost?

When properly employed, Sunday School offers everything the church needs to help believers grow in their love of God and love of one another and to grow spiritually and minister to the lost. Sunday School's effectiveness has been proven. Its design has been refined by the experience of Christians across the years and around the world.

But what about Sunday School as a means to help people grown and develop as disciples? The Sunday School offers the church an *effective and efficient design.* It is designed as a small-group Bible study based on age and development. It provides systematic Bible study that leads believers to a greater understanding of God and their own spiritual life, a burden for the lost, and a love for the family of God. The Sunday School brings believers into close contact and provides an effective vehicle for newcomer and absentee follow-up and care. The age-graded small group is the ideal place to welcome and assimilate newcomers. From all of these perspectives, the Sunday School is a magnificent disciple-making design.

Sunday School offers *practical solutions* to the challenges of disciple-making. The fundamentals of effective teaching and life-changing ministry are inherent in the Sunday School design. A wealth of excellent, high-quality teaching material is readily available for every age level, developmental task, and interest. These materials let teachers and church leaders tap the gifts, talents, and expertise of creative people who design, write, illustrate, and produce curriculum.

A wealth of training materials already exists. Dynamic programs that help teachers and workers develop their ministries are readily available. A wealth of training expertise and resources has been developed to help churches equip their workers for ministry in the Sunday School. High-quality training materials dealing with teaching methodologies, classroom management, student needs, and an array of other topics can be easily obtained. Highly trained resource people with tremendous knowledge in these areas are available to help.

Today's culture still respects Sunday as a day of worship, so a Sunday School on Sunday largely avoids school and work scheduling conflicts. Sunday School was designed more than two hundred years ago to take advantage of the rhythms of society. Since children worked six days a week, the Sunday School was a practical solution. In an agrarian society, the distance and relative difficulty of travel made combining worship and instruction on a single day very practical. Children no longer work six days a week, and travel is relatively quick and easy, but the busyness of modern life and the scheduling pressure most families face make having the Sunday School on Sunday a very practical strategy.

The Sunday School is also infinitely *adaptable.* It works equally well in small or large congregations and can be contracted or expanded to serve any church well. As the church grows, Sunday School can easily expand by adding teachers, classes, administrators, and support staff. The organizational pattern is easily adapted to fit the needs of the mega-church or the home missions church. There is no "upper limit," and there is no church too small.

Because a Sunday School class is, by definition, a teacher and a group (one or more) of learners, classes can be held almost anywhere. The ideal is for a church to have an adequate number of appropriately equipped classrooms, but Sunday School classes have been held outside under a tree, in cars, in restaurants, and on church buses. The Sunday School can be "high tech," "low tech," or "no tech." It can be held almost anytime, anywhere, and under any circumstance.

For example, my earliest Sunday School memory took place in the furnace room of a small neighborhood church. They had set up some barriers to keep us away from the boiler and created a makeshift Sunday School classroom. It was winter. The teacher's name was Hazel. I had the seat closest to the furnace. The topic for the day? Hell. It made a lasting impression.

Sunday School can adapt to meet a variety of special needs. Larger congregations have the luxury of developing highly specialized ministries to meet very specific needs. In smaller congregations the Sunday School can fulfill these same needs by creating and offering classes or electives. That flexibility lets the church address the needs of its community and members without the burden of designing and creating a new structure. That fact puts specialized ministries within the reach of almost any church.

An adult Sunday School class that reaches out to single adults, those who speak a language other than English, or those who face some special circumstance in life (for example, those whose spouses are not believers, those dealing with some life-controlling problem, those who are newly divorced) is an effective way for even the small church to minister to the needs of its community. All that is needed is leadership with a vision and a teacher with a burden. Such classes can maximize the organizational strengths of the Sunday School and provide a very effective base of ministry.

The Sunday School *interacts* well with the rest of the church. It offers the church a great "package deal." When properly designed, organized, and used, the Sunday School can not only function as the primary vehicle for instruction but also carry out a variety of other essential functions. It can be the church's infrastructure.

The Sunday School is an ideal place to keep track of absentees and newcomers. Some wonder whether taking attendance and keeping accurate records is worth the effort. They should recall that in the parable of the lost sheep, the shepherd knew how many sheep he had, when one was missing, and where to look. Good record keeping does exactly that. The Sunday School teacher knows who is supposed to be there, who's missing, and where to look for them.

The Sunday School can serve as the primary vehicle of follow-up, assimilation, and care. Sunday School teachers and workers are readily available to assist the pastor in this vital ministry. The small group nature of the Sunday School class eases the entry of new-comers into the church as they develop friends and get to know others. It's the most natural place in the church for people to feel welcomed and wanted.

The Sunday School builds unity by sharing a common under-standing of the church. Building a sense of shared identity in turn builds a sense of unity and loyalty. In Sunday School, "your church" can quickly become "our church."

The Sunday School also contributes directly to worship. The bet-ter believers know and understand God, the more likely they are to truly worship. In Sunday School, people can learn about and reflect on the magnificence of God's character, His saving grace, and His eternal love for His people. In Sunday School, people can share stories of how God has touched their lives and met their needs. It's in the Sunday School that people are most likely to find answers to their questions and discover eternal truths.

In short, the Sunday School offers, in one place and through one ministry, the essential components for healthy church devel-opment. There is no need to invent new forms of ministry or dupli-cate what Sunday School can do. Church leaders find it necessary to create new forms, not because the Sunday School design is flawed, but because it is poorly understood, implemented, and executed. Properly implemented, the Sunday School can do it all. This is especially valuable for small congregations, allowing them to concentrate their resources, energies, and efforts.

A Great Idea Badly Done

Sunday School has proven to be one of the greatest ministry tools ever developed. It has the potential to greatly enhance the life and ministry of any congregation. Again and again it has been proven an effective tool, not only of instruction, but also of church growth. Nevertheless, the Sunday School has fallen into disuse and disrepute in many churches. Why? In too many churches, the Sunday School is a great idea badly done. The failure of church leaders to recruit and train teachers and staff has resulted in poor quality of instruction. Unwillingness to commit the needed resources, facilities, material, and equipment leads to the perception that the Sunday School isn't really all that important. Neglecting to attend to organizational details essential to success results in failure. Rather than insisting on excellence, we have settled for mediocrity.

Another reason for the failure of Sunday School is the fascination many have with the new. *New* is almost always equated with *improved.* The popularity of the next new program and the relentless search in some churches for a magic bullet inevitably results in the diversion of resources, people, and attention to "hot" new ministries and away from Sunday School. Church leaders are no less susceptible to fads than the rest of the culture. Most of the time, these great new ideas boom and bust. Then leaders move on to the next ministry fad.

The proliferation of niche ministries is a third reason for this failure. Narrowly focused and highly specialized ministries are viewed as "the way to go." These inevitably absorb resources that would otherwise go to the Sunday School. They are often added without consideration of their impact on existing ministries and with little regard to a "cost/benefit" ratio.

Many church leaders have lost sight of the true potential of Sunday School as a teaching ministry and have not appreciated all the ways a good Sunday School could benefit the church. Because they don't realize the Sunday School has a potential far beyond its present application, they have not exploited its full potential.

The Right Tool

The boy loved to visit his grandfather's basement workshop. He loved the smell of sawdust and the idea of creating something of beauty and value with his own hands. Most of all, he loved just being around Grandpa.

The workshop was a veritable tool museum. The boy's grandfather had been a lifelong tool collector and had some very old and strange-looking tools. On almost every wall, the tools were neatly organized and displayed on hooks and pegboard. They were fascinating. The boy and his grandfather played a little game when they were in the workshop. The boy would stand and examine some oddly-shaped or strange-looking device and try to guess what it was used for. He almost never guessed right the first time. His grandfather would give him a clue, and he'd guess again. Guesses and clues flew back and forth until the exasperated boy gave up.

Then the boy's grandfather would take the tool in his hands and explain what the tool did, why it was designed the way it was, and how to properly use it. Once the boy understood its use, the design was obvious.

Once they were in the middle of a project and the boy's grandfather needed to cut a board. Surrounding him were a variety of specialty saws—a table saw, a jigsaw, several different circular saws, a coping saw, a miter saw in the miter box, and several others. But what he reached for was an old and well-used (but well-cared-for) handsaw. In his grandfather's skilled hands, the saw's sharp teeth quickly cut through the board. The job was done. The cut was straight and smooth.

As the boy watched, it dawned on him that his grandfather could have used a circular saw or even set up the table saw to make that cut, but either would have taken longer to get out and set up than using the handsaw. It would have been almost impossible to make that cut with a jigsaw, coping saw, miter saw, or pruning saw. None of them was the right tool for the job, but that old handsaw did the trick.

The boy's grandfather seemed to read his mind. (He did that a lot.) He gave the boy a knowing wink, a broad grin, and a timely bit of advice: "Sometimes the old ways are the best ways."

The Sunday School can, like a well-used tool in the hands of a skilled craftsman, be the right tool for the job. Sometimes the old ways are the best ways.

Endnotes

[1] "Lady Be Good: Recovery in 1959 of B-24 crew lost in Libyan Desert in 1943", www.qmfound.com/lady_be_good_b-24_bomber_recovery.htm

The Sunday School Teacher: Mentor and Friend

Mentor and Telemachus

Before it was a title, Mentor was a name.

Before it was a teaching technique, Mentor was a man.

Here's the story.

The *Iliad* and the *Odyssey,* Homer's great epic poems, tell the story of the Trojan wars and Odysseus's journey home. Homer introduces Odysseus, king of Ithaca, not as the hero he became, but as a draft dodger who pretended to be insane so he and his kingdom wouldn't have to join the alliance against Troy. To prove Odysseus sane, Palamedes put Odysseus's infant son, Telemachus, in front of his father's plow. When Odysseus swerved to avoid his son, he lost his excuse and sealed his fate.

Odysseus left his wife, Penelope, and Telemachus in the care of his elderly servant and trusted friend, Mentor. When Odysseus sailed for Troy, no one realized how long he would be gone. He fought for ten years before the Trojans rolled that wooden horse into their city. His journey home took another ten years. Mentor stood by his oath and taught Telemachus, by word and by deed, the ways of a civilized man. For twenty years Mentor was a faithful and trustworthy counselor, friend, and teacher to Telemachus.

The story of Odysseus, Mentor, and Telemachus takes an unusual twist. Athena, the goddess of war, took special interest in young Telemachus, sometimes taking the form of Mentor to advise and assist him. When Telemachus was unable to resist his mother's suitors, Athena, in the form of Mentor, urged him to stand up to them and order them to leave. When that failed, Athena, again in the form of Mentor, prompted Telemachus to find his father, and she accompanied him on his journeys. Mentor advised Telemachus to return to Ithaca by another route and avoid an ambush set by Penelope's suitors. When no other means of escape could be found, Mentor leaped with Telemachus into the sea from a high cliff on Calypso's island and they swam to their ship.

When Telemachus returned to Ithaca, he was a changed man. The hesitant and timid boy had been transformed. The infant son Odysseus left behind had grown into a brave, honest, respectful, and respectable man—all thanks to Mentor. This mature and courageous son joined his father in defeating his mother's suitors and returning Odysseus to the throne of Ithaca.

That's just Greek mythology. But this ancient tutor's name has become our word for a wise, trusted, and faithful friend, counselor, and teacher.

Introduction

What is a teacher?

There are two very different ways to think about the role of the teacher.

The Teacher as Expert

Some see teachers as resident experts whose primary task is to transfer their knowledge and understanding to their students.

Much of secular and Christian education is built on this model. Teachers are to know their subject and be skilled communicators. Students (or their parents) choose schools based on the academic acumen of the faculty, who expect their students to master their subjects. The educational institution is structured to support this notion. In high schools, colleges, and universities, students move through the system taking courses. Even in preschools and elementary schools, time is set aside to focus on specific content. Technologies, whether written, visual, or audio, are employed to better communicate content.

Schools and teachers are judged by their ability to transfer information to their students. Students succeed or fail based on their mastery of content. Schools become an assembly line of information in which students move along a conveyor belt of courses with each successive teacher adding his or her part until the student is a finished product. The students roll off this assembly line, are handed a diploma, and are assured that they are ready for whatever comes next.

Several things should be noted. This model can be an extremely effective and efficient way to deliver a lot of information to a lot of students, but the relationship between teacher and student is relatively insignificant in the process. It doesn't matter whether or not a teacher likes or is interested in his or her students as people. What matters is how well the teacher delivers content. It doesn't matter whether the students like or value the teacher. What matters most is that students get what they pay for—mastery of the subject and a diploma or degree.

In this approach information is king. The underlying assumption is that a change in knowledge automatically leads to a change in attitude and that change in attitude will in turn automatically lead to a change in behavior. The way to influence students and their conduct is to effectively and efficiently communicate accurate information. There is only one problem: It doesn't work that way.

This perspective profoundly impacts how teachers understand their role and what learners expect of their teachers. Their obligation begins and ends at the classroom door. Students often share that perspective. Their relationship with the teacher is almost always and exclusively related to the subject matter and the classroom experience.

This view has become the dominant educational model. It has proven to be an excellent way to create knowledge and communicate information and understanding. But not all of life can be reduced to an academic exercise. This kind of education has serious limitations when it is used in the church. There is a vast difference between knowing and doing what's right, between understanding ethics and being ethical, and between knowing about God and knowing God. It may be a great way to communicate information, but information alone is insufficient for successful Christian living.

Finally, there is no doubt that this dominant, secular educational model has been baptized and brought lock, stock, and chalkboard into the church. The world's educational models have been and are being replicated in the church without thought of whether this kind of teaching is the best way to help people grow in their faith. We assume it is and act on that assumption.

Many have accepted the notion that effectively and efficiently communicating biblical information is the most important thing they can do. They determine what will be taught and in what order, establish age-grade classes, and offer electives to our teens and adults. They do so because this model of education is the model with which most are familiar. Secular education has developed highly effective and efficient ways to teach, and church leaders want the very best for their teachers and learners. We have accepted the secular model because we believe it is better.

But is it?

The Teacher as Mentor

The second way to view the teacher is as a wise and trusted friend, guide, and mentor. These teachers are wise. They know the Bible and how to teach, but they are concerned with far more than just efficiently and effectively delivering information. They want their students to understand the meaning and significance of the Bible and how it relates to their lives. Applying the Bible's truths in daily living and in relating to all of life is critical to learning and to their role as teachers. These teachers aren't interested in simply providing information. They are interested in helping their students develop truly Christian lifestyles that integrate and express biblical learning in every aspect of their lives.

This way to teach the Bible can best be illustrated by four questions every student should be able to answer at the end of a Sunday School class.

What does the Bible say?

What does the Bible mean?

What does the Bible mean to me?

What am I going to do about it?

Next, these teachers listen to and understand how their students think and feel. Mentors know that real learning and growth are processes that involve much more than the acquisition of new knowledge. Real learning demands that students reflect on, question, and challenge what they are taught. Real learning takes place in the crucible of applying the biblical truth and reflecting on that experience. Inevitably it feels like a trial-and-error process with many failures and successes, frustrations and victories. Great teachers willingly walk through this process with their students, listen to their stories, and encourage them to listen to one another. They help students make sense of their experience, point the way to the next step, turn stumbling blocks into stepping-stones, warn of obstacles, pick learners up when then fall, and encourage and motivate learners to achieve even greater things in their lives and ministries.

These teachers understand that their relationship with their students and the relationships students develop with one another are at the core of a real learning process. These relationships are not a distraction from "real" learning. The message can never be divorced from the messenger. The way students relate to their teachers and their feelings about the teaching-learning process changes the way they understand and feel about what is being taught. Knowing this, wise mentors teach with an eye on the relational quality of their teaching. They teach people, not lessons. Forging healthy relationships based on mutual respect and concern is essential for successful teaching.

Wise teachers know that their responsibilities don't end at the classroom (or church) door; they begin there. Mentors are involved in their students' lives outside the classroom. They understand that their example is as much a part of their teaching as their words. Their conduct, words, and lifestyle are inextricably linked to their teaching. They know they are being watched. Discrepancies between what they teach and how they live will certainly bring disrepute to the gospel and disrespect for the teacher, and they will disrupt the student's spiritual growth and development. Mentors "walk the walk," not just "talk the talk."

Purpose and Process

Which path should a Sunday School teacher follow?

The only way to choose the path is to determine the purpose of our teaching. Clearly many churches and church leaders have already chosen the secular model and its emphasis on delivering information. But that begs the question: Do Christian education and secular education share the same purpose?

The answer must be a resounding and absolute "No!" Effectively and efficiently communicating biblical and doctrinal information can never be the only focus of true Christian education. It's a nightmare scenario—churches full of biblically literate "pagans" who know their Bible and their doctrine but who have never experienced the life-changing power of Christ, people who know what the church teaches but don't live out those teachings in their lives, people who call themselves Christians but whose attitudes and actions are indistinguishable from their pagan neighbors. This is the way of the Pharisee and the Sadducee. They knew the teachings of the Law but not the Lawgiver. If the church chooses the same path, it will reach the same place.

Thankfully, there is another way.

Christian Education, Not Religious Instruction

The purpose of true Christian education is to transform believers from being conformed to "the pattern of this world" (Romans 12:2) to being "conformed to the likeness of his [God's] Son"(Romans 8:29)—that is, to help them become like Jesus. Christian education promotes healthy development of Christlike spirituality, character, attitudes, worldview, and behavior. This process begins with spiritual renewal through the new birth and is made possible by the presence of the Holy Spirit in the believer's life. It is intended to continue "until we all reach unity in the faith and in the knowledge of the Son of God and become mature, attaining to the whole measure of the fullness of Christ" (Ephesians 4:13).

Can an educational process designed for the effective and efficient transfer of information accomplish this goal? Of course not! It's not designed to. It's designed to impact a person's understanding but doesn't necessarily address other critical dimensions of spiritual growth. Is knowing and understanding the Bible and our doctrine essential to spiritual growth and development? Absolutely! Is it, by itself, sufficient for the task? Absolutely not! James reminds us that even the demons know the truth and tremble (James 2:19). The church must take full advantage of every opportunity to improve the teaching-learning process, exploiting every technique and technology to its full potential to improve communication of the Bible's message. We should be the best. After all, we teach eternal truths that impact eternal destinies.

The church must always remember that biblical information alone isn't enough. It is the beginning of the process. The church should not eliminate the excellent educational infrastructure it has created. Most of it is valuable and can be used to help people become like Jesus. But the church must use those tools to further the purposes of the gospel. Other essential elements needed to help our learners become fully devoted followers of Jesus must be added to the process.

The secular model also fails because it is not the biblical model. Our educational structures and institutions are the creation of our Western culture and society; they are not based on biblical models. The Bible is not silent about the teaching-learning process, but its vision is vastly different from our modern, Western paradigm of education. At the heart of biblical teaching is the relationship between teacher and student, between master and disciple. The Bible views the teacher as mentor and friend. Biblical examples of these relationships include Moses and Joshua, Elijah and Elisha, Jesus and the Twelve, and Paul and Timothy. We can see examples of mentoring in Barnabas taking the church's first and perhaps greatest persecutor, Paul, under his wing and in Aquila and Priscilla welcoming the brash young Apollos into their lives.

The pattern is clear and repeated throughout the New Testament. Here are examples of biblical mentors in action.

> I have been reminded of your sincere faith, which first lived in your grandmother Lois and in your mother Eunice and, I am persuaded, now lives in you also (2 Timothy 1:5).

> You then, my son, be strong in the grace that is in Christ Jesus. And the things you have heard me say in the presence of many witnesses entrust to reliable men who will also be qualified to teach others (2 Timothy 2:1,2).

Likewise, teach the older women . . . Then they can train the younger women (Titus 2:3,4).

Similarly, encourage the young men to be self-controlled. In everything set them an example by doing what is good. In your teaching show integrity, seriousness and soundness of speech that cannot be condemned (Titus 2:6–8).

Let's be clear. This isn't an "either-or" proposition. The church does not have to choose between effective biblical instruction and mentoring relationships. In fact, it must not choose. No information delivery technique or technology, no matter how efficient or effective, can replace a true mentor and friend in the life of the learner. But mentors must effectively and accurately communicate biblical truth. A believer's healthy spiritual development demands the active involvement of other believers. Spiritual growth is a relational process that involves the believer in a dynamic relationship not only with God but with other Christians as well.

An information-based model fails because it does not address the needs of the church. Real Christian education doesn't just create a place where believers gain new information; it creates an environment in which the individual believer can grow and contribute to the healthy growth of the body of believers. Its purpose isn't just the healthy development of the individual believer; it is also the healthy development of the church. Paul wrote, "It was he [Christ] who gave some to be apostles, some to be prophets, some to be evangelists, and some to be pastors and teachers, to prepare God's people for works of service, so that the body of Christ may be built up until we all reach unity in the faith" (Ephesians 4:11–13).

Adding to a person's stockpile of biblical information doesn't necessarily contribute to the creation of a healthy body of believers, because it cannot, in and of itself, contribute to the healthy development of individual believers. Church unity isn't just about doctrinal agreement. Rancorous church fights and splits often involve believers who share the same biblical understandings and perspectives. Rather, true unity is built through the bonds of affection and personal relationships. Bible study classes that are gatherings of strangers dutifully taking in whatever biblical content the teacher puts out don't build unity. Learners may share a particular understanding, but they never become a truly united body of believers.

The bonds of unity are not just doctrinal; they are relational. The believer's love for and loyalty to God and other believers is the cement holding the church together. John wrote:

> This is the message we have heard from him and declare to you: God is light; in him there is no darkness at all. If we claim to have fellowship with him yet walk in the darkness, we lie and do not live by the truth. But if we walk in the light, as he is in the light, we have fellowship with one another, and the blood of Jesus, his Son, purifies us from all sin . . . . Anyone who claims to be in the light but hates his brother is still in the darkness. Whoever loves his brother lives in the light, and there is nothing in him to make him stumble. But whoever hates his brother is in the darkness and walks around in the darkness (1 John 1:5–7; 2:9–11).

Healthy, strong relationships don't just happen. They aren't the automatic result of sitting in a classroom or sanctuary and hearing the exposition of God's Word. Relationships grow when believers know one another, care about one another, and share their lives. They are the result of shared actions and interactions, not just shared understandings.

Seven Insights From the Bible's Great Mentors

Each of the Bible's great mentors is unique, but they all shared and applied the same fundamental principles and practices. Many of these are illustrated in the powerful relationship between Elijah and Elisha.

First, mentors cannot give what they do not first possess. In the account of the passing of Elijah's cloak (2 Kings 2), Elijah could give Elisha the cloak because he had it. Teachers must first possess in themselves the qualities they wish to see replicated in their learners. Thus, the first task of mentors is to develop their own walk with God, grow in their understanding of God and His ways, develop spiritual disciplines in their own lives, and genuinely reflect the image of the Master. An old saying goes, "We teach what we know. We reproduce what we are."

Great mentors help their learners focus on what is most important. Elijah asked Elisha specifically what he could do for him (2 Kings 2:9). Elisha knew Elijah would soon be gone; it was his last chance. The importance of the moment wasn't wasted on Elisha. Surely, he raced through the options in his mind but chose what is most important—God's blessing and presence. Wise mentors keep the most important things at the forefront of their teaching. Jesus, the ultimate mentor, admonished, "Do not worry, saying, 'What shall we eat?' or 'What shall we drink?' or 'What shall we wear?' For the pagans run after all these things, and your heavenly Father knows that you need them. But seek first his kingdom and his righteousness, and all these things will be given to you as well" (Matthew 6:31–33).

Paul too demonstrated a clear focus on the important. "One thing I do: Forgetting what is behind and straining toward what is ahead, I press on toward the goal to win the prize for which God has called me heavenward in Christ Jesus" (Philippians 3:13,14).

Great mentors also challenge and encourage their students to press on and go further than they ever thought they could. Three times Elijah suggested that Elisha stay behind. Three times Elisha refused and pressed forward with his master (2 Kings 2:1–6). It may appear that Elijah was trying to discourage his disciple or that Elisha was disrespectful and disobedient. Instead, Elijah's questions capture a spiritual reality. When a disciple achieves a spiritual plateau, the temptation is to stay put. Elijah was clear that there were new heights to reach and he intended to go on. Clearly, Elisha chose to take his journey's next step. So must we.

Three times Jesus asked Peter, "Do you love me?" (John 21:15–17). And Paul encouraged his fellow soldier Archippus (Philemon 1:2) to press on in his calling until it was completed. He wrote, "Tell Archippus: 'See to it that you complete the work you have received in the Lord' " (Colossians 4:17).

Wise mentors demonstrate in their lives the principles and practices they teach. Elijah demonstrated the use of the cloak. When Elisha's turn came, he duplicated his master's actions with identical results (2 Kings 2:7,8,14). Jesus taught His disciples to pray by praying. As a wise mentor, Paul could encourage the church at Corinth to do as he did. "Follow my example, as I follow the example of Christ. I praise you for remembering me in everything and for holding to the teachings, just as I passed them on to you" (1 Corinthians 11:1,2).

Mentors not only learn the disciplines of the spiritual life but also learn to discipline themselves. Knowing that others follow their example, they realize what is at stake and stay in control of their attitudes, words, and deeds. Paul wrote, "Therefore I do not run like a man running aimlessly; I do not fight like a man beating the air. No, I beat my body and make it my slave so that after I have preached to others, I myself will not be disqualified for the prize" (1 Corinthians 9:26,27).

Elijah demonstrated that he was a wise mentor when he established a close and ongoing relationship with Elisha. Elisha didn't just show up for a prophetic seminar and go home; he stayed with Elijah in a close personal relationship. For Elisha to receive the cloak, he had to be with Elijah when he was translated (2 Kings 2:10). Jesus demonstrated the same principle in the calling of the Twelve. "He appointed twelve—designating them apostles—that they might be with him and that he might send them out to preach" (Mark 3:14).

The ministry of these twelve was predicated as much on the fact that they had been with Jesus as on what they had learned from Jesus. When Peter and John were arrested in Jerusalem after the Day of Pentecost, it was their relationship with Jesus that caught their accusers off guard. "When they saw the courage of Peter and John and realized that they were unschooled, ordinary men, they were astonished and they took note that these men had been with Jesus" (Acts 4:13).

Moses mentored Joshua for more than forty years. Jesus spent three years with the Twelve. Paul spent three years in Damascus learning from the brothers before beginning his ministry. He spent years with Barnabas and then invested years in Timothy, Silas, Philemon, and many others.

Mentors hold their disciples accountable for their actions, confronting them when necessary, but they don't give up on them. We see this demonstrated in Paul's relationship with John Mark.

> When Barnabas and Saul had finished their mission, they returned from Jerusalem, taking with them John, also called Mark (Acts 12:25).

> Barnabas wanted to take John, also called Mark, with them, but Paul did not think it wise to take him, because he had deserted them in Pamphylia and had not continued with them in the work. They had such a sharp disagreement that they parted company. Barnabas took Mark and sailed for Cyprus, but Paul chose Silas and left, commended by the brothers to the grace of the Lord (Acts 15:37–40).

Paul held John Mark accountable for his actions, but Barnabas refused to give up on a promising young disciple who had made a mistake. In the long run, both were proven right. Years later Paul celebrated the investment in the one who deserted them at Pamphylia. He wrote to Timothy, "Only Luke is with me. Get Mark and bring him with you, because he is helpful to me in my ministry" (2 Timothy 4:11). And to Philemon he wrote, "Epaphras, my fellow prisoner in Christ Jesus, sends you greetings. And so do Mark, Aristarchus, Demas and Luke, my fellow workers" (1:23,24).

Finally, great mentors are great learners. Often they are being mentored while mentoring others. Moses received good advice from his father-in-law, Jethro (Exodus 18), while he was taking the young Joshua and Caleb under his wing. Paul went to Jerusalem to seek the guidance of the apostles (Acts 9:26–30) and returned to Jerusalem after a missionary journey to seek again the wisdom and blessing of the elders (Acts 15). Paul, who learned from his mentor, Barnabas, mentored John Mark, Silas, Timothy, and others.

From Religious Instruction to Christian Education

Shifting Sunday School from an educational ministry focused on information to one built on mentoring relationships means changes in structure and organization involving both leadership and teachers.

Structure and Organization

What does it take to create an environment in which a mentoring style of Christian education can take place?

First, leaders and teachers must value their existing structures and organization. Just because effectively communicating biblical and doctrinal truth isn't everything doesn't mean it is nothing. The curricula, technologies, organization, and structures that support the instructional process should be kept and enhanced as long as they do not interfere with or work against the purposes of spiritual growth and development and as long as they contribute to the effective communication of God's Word.

Applying several key principles to the Sunday School will help to make the transition.

A. Appropriate Student-Teacher Ratios

It is impossible for teachers to develop mentoring relationships if they are overwhelmed by large numbers of students. The following student-teacher ratios (based on average attendance, not enrollment) make mentoring relationships possible.[1]

Preschool	one teacher for every five students
Elementary	one teacher for every six to eight students
Youth	one teacher for every eight students
Adult	one teacher/group leader for every ten students

Some think such small class size is impossible. It isn't. The fact that so many teachers are overwhelmed with large numbers of students is a barrier to recruiting and to reducing the number of students per teacher. Teachers who have too many students often feel they are just baby-sitting or running crowd control. Limiting class size improves the experience for teachers and learners, making it easier to recruit adequate staff. It also promotes an atmosphere of growth, is essential to relational teaching, and helps transform chaotic classrooms into places of joyful discovery and exciting learning.

Youth and adult classes often have larger numbers of students. In such cases classes should be organized with internal small groups of eight to ten students with a group leader who assists the teacher and becomes a mentor and friend to members of their small group.

B. Accurate Records

Gathering and keeping accurate records for all class members, newcomers, and visitors may seem mundane, but it is a critical step in the mentoring process. Records should include accurate and up-to-date contact information (address, phone, e-mail, and so on), pertinent personal information (birthdays, anniversaries, and other important dates), family information (parents, spouse, children, etc.), and accurate attendance records.

This information should not only be collected; it should be used. Contacting absent members to see if they have a need or concern demonstrates care. Calling newcomers and visitors to thank them for attending and to extend a warm welcome demonstrates care and concern. Noticing important dates in a person's life with a phone call, card, note, or e-mail message bolsters a student's sense of value and inclusion. All of these steps build the essential relationship between teachers and their learners, and none of them are possible without accurate and current records.

C. Instructional Methodology

The way teachers teach teaches as much as what they teach. Many teachers rely almost solely on storytelling (for children) or lecture (for youth and adults). Such reliance is understandable. It is the way most have experienced education. It fits our cultural and experiential paradigm of education as the process by which an expert communicates information about a subject to learners. It also fits our church experience. After all, a sermon is one form of a lecture. For skilled lecturers or storytellers, it is the easiest way to teach. It's also easy for the student. It demands so little—just sit still and listen.

Overuse of lecture, however, works against the development of mentoring relationships. Its one-way communication permits little or no feedback. Lecturers never really know what their students think or feel. They don't even know for sure if the learners are listening and actually hearing what they say.

The classroom must shift from a model in which the teacher is an active teller and students are passive listeners/receivers. Participatory learning in which both teacher and learner are active should take its place. Ample time should be allowed for students to respond to and discuss the biblical truths they are exploring. Teaching techniques like question and answer, research and reporting, small-group discussion, role-play, and many others are ways to make the classroom a lively place where people discover God's truth for themselves and interact with one another.

Incorporating learning activities that are age appropriate and specifically designed to encourage students to interact and get to know one another is another critical step in the process. Planning for and allowing time for fellowship as students arrive and taking time to share prayer requests and testimonies enhance the relational environment.

D. Facilities and Room Arrangement

The physical environment can enhance or inhibit the relational quotient of the class. Here are some practical suggestions:

1. Greet all students as they arrive by positioning a "welcome station" at the door.
2. Arrange seating so students see not only the teacher but also one another. Some classes can gather around tables. In other settings arrange chairs in circles or horseshoes of six to eight. If there is fixed seating, give opportunity for people to stand or turn around and interact with others in the class.
3. If appropriate, place a snack area in the classroom as a place at which students can gather and interact with one another.

Leadership Responsibilities

Those leading the church's educational ministry play a critical role. Here are some practical suggestions for pastors, Sunday School superintendents, Christian Education directors, and other leaders.

A. Set the "Bench Mark"

Leadership must clearly establish and communicate what is expected of Sunday School teachers. Clearly explaining the priority, principles, and process of mentoring is a critical first step. It's an important beginning, not an end.

B. Teach and Train

Teachers teach the way they were taught. Most understand their role and responsibilities in light of their own educational experiences in school and at church. Some are natural mentors; most are not. But all of them can and should be trained and helped so they can acquire the skills needed for effective mentoring. The best way to train teachers to mentor is for leadership to mentor them and model the principles and practices of effective relational teaching. It doesn't make sense to train teachers to mentor by presenting a good lecture on mentoring.

C. Build the Organization

Keeping student-teacher ratios small and building an effective record-keeping system that supports teachers' mentoring relationships with their students are important ways leaders can build the organization.

Another critical leadership task is creating an effective recruiting and training strategy that brings into ministry sufficient numbers of qualified and trained teachers, leaders, and support staff.

Finally, leaders can and should create an organizational system built on mentoring principles in which department superintendents establish the same kinds of mentoring relationships with their teachers and staff that they expect the teachers to establish with their students.

D. Establish Accountability

An old saying goes, "A lot more of what's inspected gets done than what's expected." Accountability doesn't have to be onerous or heavy-handed. It certainly should never be a power trip. Accountability is an integral part of any effective organization. It is a simple matter of determining what should be done, establishing a way to do it, asking whether it was done as expected, and responding appropriately. For instance, teachers should contact absent members. Cards, phone calls, e-mails, or visits are all appropriate depending on the situation. This expectation should be clearly articulated. Somebody should ask whether the contact was made in accordance with the standards. If it was, then appropriate recognition and expressions of appreciation are definitely in order. If it wasn't, then a gentle reminder, additional training and support, or other steps are needed.

The Teacher's Task

Mentoring ultimately comes down to teachers' relationships with their students. No amount of organizational excellence or leadership support will matter if teachers don't change the way they teach. Here are ten steps to better relational teaching.

1. Teach students, not lessons. Understand what students need, and remember that their lives are the most important concern.
2. Build healthy relationships with all students. Demonstrate interest in their lives. Discover their gifts and talents. Listen to their stories. Care about their lives.
3. Make time and take time in the class for relationship building. Use activities and teaching techniques that give your students the opportunity to talk with you and with one another. Take time for prayer requests and testimonies.
4. Move to a participatory teaching style. Lecture or tell stories only in moderation. Use techniques like small-group discussion, question and answer, and research and reporting not only to improve learning but also to help develop relationships.
5. Treat your learners with care and respect inside and outside the classroom.
6. Build systems that demonstrate you care. Collect needed information. Mark significant days and occasions with a card, phone call, e-mail, or better yet, your presence. Make sure that when they are absent, they know they were missed.
7. Develop a relationship outside the classroom. Visit students at school or go to their activities, such as athletic events or concerts. Invite the class to your house for dessert after church. Plan fun activities that help build friendships. Involve the class in service and ministry projects that provide opportunities for students to get to know you in other ways.
8. Let students get to know you, your family, and your life. Don't be a stranger.
9. We all leave trails in our lives that others follow. Be sure yours are worth following.
10. Don't be afraid to lovingly confront and challenge your students to be better, do more, and discover and develop their God-given gifts and abilities.

It's not possible for every Sunday School teacher to establish a close mentoring relationship with every student. But if every Sunday School teacher tries to do so, every student will have the opportunity to respond. It is possible that every student will find at least one teacher willing to be his or her wise counselor, friend, and guide—willing to be a mentor.

Conclusion

It is hard to estimate just how important a teacher can be in the life of a student. Charlie Rose graduated from high school in 1901. He was undeniably the teacher's pet. When Charlie graduated he was class valedictorian, editor of the yearbook and had a number of other outstanding accomplishments. At graduation Charlie's teacher, Miss Tillie Brown, congratulated Charlie, but none of her other students, with a rose and a polite kiss on his cheek.

Not surprisingly, Miss Brown's other students were disappointed that they had not received the same kind of congratulations. A delegation of the disappointed sent one of their number to ask why they had been so neglected. Miss Brown stood firm. She said that Charlie had earned her special recognition, and that if they did something truly worthwhile, they too would get a kiss.

Charlie went on to distinguish himself and was ultimately handpicked by President Harry Truman as his press secretary. His first duty was to carry a message to Miss Tillie Brown from the president of the United States. The message said:

Dear Miss Brown,
How about the kiss I never got? Have I done something worthwhile enough to earn it now?

Harry S Truman
President of the United States

Truman got his kiss—the kiss he didn't receive the night he and Charlie Rose graduated from the same high school in

Independence, Missouri; the night he confronted Miss Brown on behalf of all those disappointed students; the night she challenged him to do something worthwhile with his life.[2]

Endnotes

[1]Lowell Brown, ed., *Sunday School Standards* (Ventura, Calif.: Gospel Light Publications, 1980), 50–9.

[2]Paul Aurandt, ed., *Paul Harvey's The Rest of the Story* (New York: Doubleday, 1977), 113, 114.

The Sunday School Teacher: Evangelist and Assimilator

A Nobody Named Kimball

Edward Kimball was a Sunday School teacher concerned about one of his young students who worked in a shoe store. One day Kimball visited the student at the store and found him in the back stocking shoes. Kimball led him to Christ then and there. That young student, Dwight L. Moody, eventually left the shoe store to become one of the greatest preachers and evangelists of all time.

A young man named J. Wilbur Chapman attended one of Moody's meetings in Chicago. There Moody counseled Chapman which helped him to receive certainty of his salvation. In later years, Chapman and Moody became friends and worked together.

Chapman went on to become one of the most effective evangelists of his time. A volunteer by the name of Billy Sunday helped set up his crusades and learned how to preach by watching Chapman. Billy Sunday became one of the most dynamic evangelists of the twentieth century. In the great arenas of the nation, Billy Sunday's preaching turned thousands of people to Christ.

Inspired by a 1924 Billy Sunday crusade in Charlotte, North Carolina, a committee of Christians dedicated themselves to reach that city for Christ. That committee invited evangelist Mordecai Ham to hold a series of evangelistic meetings in 1934. A lanky sixteen-year-old sat in the huge crowd one evening, spellbound by the message of the white-haired preacher who seemed to be shouting and waving his finger at him alone. Night after night the teenager attended and finally went forward to give his life to Christ.

The teenager? Billy Graham—the man who has undoubtedly communicated the gospel of Jesus Christ to more people than any other man in history.[1]

Remember how this sequence started? A "nobody" named Edward Kimball, concerned for one of his Sunday School students, visited him at a shoe store—and in that simple act, he changed the world. Millions of people have been affected by his decision to share the gospel with just one person. And millions more continue to feel the impact of that one act.

Now nearing the end of his life and ministry, Billy Graham not only has seen millions come to Christ, but also has established a great evangelistic association and a training center for evangelists on a major seminary campus. He also has inspired and helped launch the ministries of countless pastors, missionaries, and other evangelists. They will write the next chapter of Edward Kimball's story.

Can anything like that happen today? Certainly! God wants to use each of us to change our world.

Introduction

Edward Kimball set off a chain reaction of gospel and grace that reverberates through time and literally around the world. It is inconceivable that Kimball understood the full import or impact of his simple act. What an exciting and thrilling story! But it is not at all an unusual story. Throughout the church's nearly two thousand –year history, that same story has been told over and over again on every continent and in every language. The gospel moves forward through time in an ever-widening circle as one life touches another and that life in turn touches others.

That's the plan. It always has been the plan.

Following Christ's crucifixion, death, and resurrection, His disciples faced an uncertain future. Before the events of that first Easter, their future seemed certain. They would follow their rabbi into the halls of power and the palaces of Judea when He expelled the Roman conquerors and their collaborators. After that first Easter, they weren't sure what to do. Most of them, Peter included, returned to their former lives and occupations. But Jesus had other plans.

> Then the eleven disciples went to Galilee, to the mountain where Jesus had told them to go. When they saw him, they worshiped him; but some doubted. Then Jesus came to them and said, 'All authority in heaven and on earth has been given to me. Therefore go and make disciples of all nations, baptizing them in the name of the Father and of the Son and of the Holy Spirit, and teaching them to obey everything I have commanded you. And surely I am with you always, to the very end of the age' (Matthew 28:16–20).

Jesus clearly linked evangelism and instruction in an unbreakable bond. He intended that a seamless flow from proclamation and conversion to instruction, obedience, and incorporation into the body of Christ develop in the life and ministry of the church. Evangelism, instruction, and assimilation are not separate functions; they are part and parcel of the same process: disciple-making.

In our time, however, the church has tended to see these as separate functions and to segment its ministry into distinct categories. The hope is that somehow the evangelists will hand off their converts to the educators and that somehow the educators will pass their students to an assimilation process. In our assembly line society, it seems to make sense. But if the handoff doesn't happen, if those responsible for one part of the process fail, then the whole disciple-making system collapses. While better than no plan at all, this approach falls woefully short.

The history of modern evangelistic efforts inside and outside the church is marked by this failure. Citywide evangelistic crusades are held and hundreds or even thousands of conversions reported. But often there is little or no increase in the number attending local congregations. Local congregations hold evangelistic events, and people come to Christ. Weeks or months later, many, if not all, of these converts are gone. The handoff doesn't happen, and new converts slip through the cracks. It's not for lack of good intentions or hard work. It's just the wrong plan.

The result of evangelism without follow-up is disastrous for the church. The church isn't ultimately interested in names on a decision card. Rather, the church presents the gospel so that people can become fully devoted followers of Jesus Christ and inherit eternal life. Watching new believers fall away is heartbreaking and demoralizing. It is a painful reminder of the church's failure to fulfill its purpose and carry out our Lord's most important command.

The Church—Reaching and Keeping

Evangelism is three-dimensional. *First, the church exists to proclaim the gospel to those who have not yet believed and seeks to bring people to Christ.* Confronting nonbelievers with their need for a Savior, clearly proclaiming Christ's life-giving death and resurrection, and giving nonbelievers the opportunity to receive the grace of Christ through faith are all essential steps. Crusades, altar calls, and a variety of other evangelistic events are designed to carry out this vital function.

Beyond sponsoring evangelistic events, the church seeks to be a witness in the community and in the world. Feeding the hungry, providing clothing and shelter for those in need, visiting those in prison or confined to their homes or convalescent centers, and ministering through other activities are all ways the church bears witness to Christ and His work.

Preparing believers to do evangelistic work is a second critical task of the church and its leaders. Believers must understand that bringing the gospel to the lost and dying is their personal responsibility. They must feel compassion for the lost they know and the lost they have never met. They must be taught to support missions at home and around the world as well as the evangelistic efforts of their local congregation.

Believers need to be prepared to share the gospel personally with family, friends, coworkers, and others who do not know Christ. Most believers want to share their faith but feel ill-equipped for the task. Preparing believers to share their faith effectively and lead others to Christ is central to the eternal purposes of the Church in the world. Failure to equip believers for evangelism leads to their failure to fulfill God's will for their lives and to the Church's failure to fulfill the Great Commission.

Finally, the task of evangelism is incomplete if new believers aren't brought into the life and fellowship of the church and helped to become fully devoted followers of Christ. *Incorporation, assimilation, and instruction form the third dimension of evangelism.*

Complete integration into the local body of believers is essential to the new believer's growth and development. Like a newborn infant, the newborn believer needs the help, support, and nourishment others provide. Without it they cannot survive. Developing relationships and support systems is essential.

First, assimilation capitalizes on the power of relationships. These relationships form a *support system* essential for survival in the inevitable times of trial and turmoil believers face. These relationships foster a sense of belonging. They create a *family.* That sense of family in turn helps shape a sense of *identity.* New believers move from believing that Jesus is the Messiah to believing *in* Jesus. Ultimately that belief forms the basis for their sense of self. No longer do they

93

just believe that Jesus is the Christ or just believe in Him. They are Christians. All of life's decisions and actions flow from the sense of self.

The assimilation process provides an environment for healthy growth and development. Involving new believers in the life of the church exposes them to the presence of God in Spirit-filled worship. They hear the anointed preaching. Spiritual growth and development become possible as they are engaged in the systematic study of God's Word in Sunday School. The bonds of fellowship are strengthened as they experience the love, care, and concern of fellow believers. Their love of the church and its people and leaders as well as their loyalty to the cause of Christ are cemented. Their roots sink deep into the church from which they draw all they need to grow into the fullness of Christ.

Evangelism, Assimilation, and the Sunday School

There has long been a myth that Sunday School is ineffective in attracting the unchurched. However, recent study indicates otherwise:

> But our research has shown the resurgence of Sunday School in the more effective churches in America. Further more we learned . . . that the formerly unchurched are positive and attracted to Sunday School. In fact the formerly unchurched were more likely to be active in Sunday School than the transfer church . . . a formerly unchurched . . . man . . . expressed the views of many . . .: "Look, I'm a new Christian. I've got so much to learn. What better place to learn and to fellowship with other Christians than a Sunday School class?"
>
> We did notice a slight transition from the nomenclature "Sunday School" . . . because of the churches perception of how the name "Sunday School" is received. None of the formerly unchurched expressed concerns about the name.[2]

The Sunday School offers the church a cohesive and comprehensive system of evangelism and assimilation as well as instruction.

The Sunday School offers a highly trained and motivated core of believers already committed to the life and ministry of the church. It is a short step for teachers, secretaries, department leaders, and the rest of the Sunday School staff to focus on outreach and assimilation. Sunday School already has learners who are eager to share their faith and who can be challenged, trained, and motivated to bring friends, family, coworkers, and neighbors to Christ.

The Sunday School offers a safe place for seekers to explore the things of God. Because it ministers to every member of the family, Sunday School is an open door to the community. It is an ideal way to reach singles, seniors, moms, dads, and kids.

The Sunday School is the natural place for seekers to bring their questions and examine the claims of Christ for themselves. This pre-conversion discipling is an essential step. Conversion is a process that culminates in an act of commitment. The Sunday School teacher and class members can answer questions, lay to rest false assumptions, and give seekers the opportunity to honestly examine the claims of the gospel and their need for Christ.

Because Sunday School is a flexible organization, classes (ministries) can be created that focus on unreached groups in the community. Some of these groups are ethnic or language based. Offering a Sunday School class taught in the language of an unreached group (for example, Spanish or American Sign Language) creates an open door for evangelism. Other groups are based on commonalities. Sunday School classes for college students, single adults, single parents, the newly married, or first-time parents not only minister to specific needs but also welcome newcomers. Still other groups are based on a specific need. Short-term Sunday School classes offered to those who have lost a loved one, have recently divorced, or are struggling with some life-controlling issue or problem can touch people at a time when they are most open to the gospel and the ministry of the church.

The well-developed Sunday School offers the church an effective evangelism, follow-up, and assimilation process. The organizational structures needed to reach nonbelievers effectively and bring them into fellowship already exist in the Sunday School. Accurate record keeping, a consistent and high-quality contact strategy, and a web of social relationships can all be applied to reaching nonbelievers in the same way they are used in assimilating new believers or newcomers.

The Sunday School opens the door to personal evangelism. Teachers and students sensitive to and trained to minister to nonbelievers will have the opportunity to present the claims of Christ and ask for a response. As nonbelievers develop friendships with their Sunday School teachers and fellow class members, they become more open to Christ and are more likely to respond.

The Sunday School class is a built-in support system for new believers. Many new Christians leave the altar and return to family and friends who are not supportive and who may even be hostile. The network of concerned and caring friends developed in a Sunday School class can help get them through those rough early days and become stable in their faith. The Sunday School structure can make sure that new believers are cared for.

The Sunday School is the most logical place to train and challenge church members with the need for and the process of evangelism, assimilation, and active ministry in the church. In a Sunday School class, church members can gain the skills needed to reach nonbelievers and put those skills into practice. Sunday School leadership can engage and challenge teachers, administrators, and support staff with the importance of their ministries and explain how what they do helps reach the lost in their community.

Because the Sunday School can create new units (classes), it can become the engine of church growth. As the Sunday School grows, it can add new classes as well as specialized classes within the existing Sunday School structure. This creates space for newcomers and new believers. New units tend to grow faster than existing units. Existing classes grow to a certain size and then stop growing, and are less able to incorporate newcomers or new believers. But new classes readily reach out and incorporate new people.

Finally, the Sunday School can make sure everybody has a place and everybody is in place. People will feel they belong to a class more readily than to the church. The Sunday School also creates opportunity for service and involvement in the class and in the church. An essential part of belonging is the feeling that one is making a contribution and is a valued member of the "team." Sunday School offers places of service for people at varying levels of spiritual maturity and with different skills, gifts, and callings.

But most Sunday Schools and many churches are inward focused and primarily concerned with the needs of people who are already part of the church. What does it take to transform an "inward-focused" Sunday School into an "outward-focused" Sunday School determined to reach the world around it? How can the church and Sunday School move from a paradigm of ministry that focuses on meeting the needs of members to one that focuses on meeting the needs of those who have not yet come?

Leadership

Leadership must articulate a clear vision of the Sunday School as a ministry of evangelism and assimilation, not just instruction. Many Sunday Schools aren't in the outreach business because they do not see evangelism as their purpose or responsibility. For many, Sunday School exists only to teach believers, not to evangelize the lost. In some circles the whole notion of evangelism through the Sunday School is rejected. Some believers do not want their children, young people, or themselves exposed to and interacting with nonbelievers. They see the church as a safe haven from the world, not as a vehicle to reach the world. Therefore, leaders must lead by example and present a clear vision.

Leadership can make sure the organizational and structural basics are in place. An effective and accurate record-gathering and record-keeping system and clearly articulated follow-up procedures for which staff are held accountable are essential. Without them effective evangelism and assimilation can't happen.

Leaders can train. They must give teachers the specific skills needed to accurately present the gospel in a way consistent with the needs and abilities of their classes. They must help all those serving in the Sunday School understand how their task, whatever it is, relates to evangelism and assimilation.

Leaders can encourage and sponsor events targeted to reach unreached people and help their staff understand and maximize the outreach potential of every event. For instance, Sunday School Christmas presentations aren't just about cute kids saying cute things. They are opportunities to reach unsaved families, friends, and neighbors. The Sunday School picnic is more than burned hotdogs and sunburned kids. It is an opportunity to invite unreached family and friends, get to know them, and reach out to them with the love of Christ.

Finally, leadership can celebrate the victories. Sharing testimonies of those saved through the ministry of the Sunday School is a great way to remind the Sunday School staff and everyone else of the great job Sunday School is doing. Such recognition, when properly used, motivates and challenges every member of the church to reach those who have not yet come to Christ.

Organization and Structure

The Sunday School organization is a "natural" for outreach and assimilation, but some things can and should be done to enhance its effectiveness.

Foremost, the Sunday School should be reorganized from a "maintenance" to a "growth" mode. Classes grow to a certain point, level off, and stop growing. If a class already has more learners than the teacher can handle, the teacher is not likely to aggressively pursue visitors and newcomers. If the classroom is too small or there are no empty chairs or no place at the table, newcomers and visitors aren't likely to come back. Keeping class size in a growth mode helps keeps the Sunday School growing.

Accomplishing this goal requires several steps. First, accurate attendance records for each class must be kept, analyzed, and understood. Without accurate records there is no sure way to know if a class has reached its growth potential. Second, to capitalize on that growth momentum, leadership must create new units. If the Sunday School is growing, it is almost inevitable that classes will grow to their optimum size. At that point the process of creating a new class begins again.

Creating new classes requires that new teachers and staff are being recruited and trained before they are needed. It is impossible to create a new class if no provision is made for a new teacher. Sunday School attendance records should be analyzed so new units can be created where they are most needed. A simple way to accomplish this is to identify the month with the highest average Sunday School attendance. In many churches, this is the month in which Palm Sunday and Easter occur. Once the attendance high-water mark has been determined, the growth guidelines for student-teacher ratios can be followed to determine how many new units should be created. That in turn will determine how many teachers and other staff must be recruited and trained to support the new units. If this analysis takes place in the spring and promotion takes place in the fall, leadership has several months to prepare the staff and implement the plan.

Understanding the need and recruiting and training the staff are only part of the battle. Next, leadership must maximize its facilities. Most churches do not have all the space they would like or need. But neither do most churches get the most out of the space they have. Leaders should analyze their facility based on how many square feet each student needs. This will vary with different age groups. Space should be assigned to get the most out of the facility. Most rooms are assigned, not by this kind of process, but by tradition and convenience. Adjust the use of the facility at least annually to meet the changing needs of the Sunday School and the church.

Be willing to explore nontraditional space. Converting the fellowship hall into an open classroom in which several classes meet simultaneously can transform wasted space into useful space. Small classes can meet in offices or the church kitchen. Sometimes more than one class can meet in the sanctuary (for example, one in the choir loft, one in the balcony, and one in the pews). How about the lobby? An adult class meeting in the lobby puts unused space to work and encourages people to come on time. Consider off-site classrooms for your adults. Research meeting rooms at nearby restaurants, businesses, or schools. What about the parsonage basement or living room? Effectively using off-site classrooms is a matter of scheduling. Just start a little later and end a little sooner so class members can get back and forth to church.

Creating new units to reach specific groups within the community requires much the same process. Sunday School leadership must understand who in their community is not being reached. Leaders then determine which of those groups is most likely to respond to the ministry of the church and which of those groups the church can reach. Recruiting leadership, allocating space, and incorporating the new ministry into the Sunday School and its ministry come next. When the new class is started, leaders should make sure current church members are aware and help promote it in the community. Finally, make sure everything that can be done is done to welcome newcomers.

Utilize the record-keeping system of the church. Add any willing newcomers who live in the area and who are not active members of another congregation to your Sunday School roll on their first visit. They are now prospects, and it is the Sunday School teacher's job to reach them. Keep accurate and up-to-date contact and attendance records. Following up on absent prospects is a great way to reach them with the gospel. Don't be too quick to purge the roll. Just because people haven't yet been reached doesn't mean they can't be reached. But if they are dropped from the roll, they certainly won't be reached.

When should a person be removed from the Sunday School roll? They should be removed if they have become an active part of another congregation, if they have moved outside the church's ministry area, if they ask to be removed, or if they have died. Otherwise, keep them on the roll, keep praying for them, and keep trying to reach them.

Be sure that the welcoming process is in place and prepared to meet the needs of newcomers. Friendly greeters and ushers ready to extend a warm welcome should be in place for the Sunday School as well as morning worship. Maps of the building, a list of class offerings, literature that introduces the church and its ministries, and an opportunity to register should be readily available when newcomers arrive. Having a friendly usher to escort newcomers to their classrooms and introduce them to the teachers and others is a great help. Explaining to parents the morning schedule and where to pick up their children are ways to meet newcomers' needs.

The church never gets a second chance to make a first impression. And first impressions really are lasting impressions. If newcomers are warmly greeted and cared for from the minute they arrive on your church property, they are more likely to be receptive to the ministry of the church and to the gospel.

The Frontline of Evangelism and Assimilation: The Sunday School Teacher

Teachers are the frontline of evangelism and assimilation in the Sunday School. Success or failure initiates with them. No amount of restructuring and reorganization by leadership can succeed if teachers don't reach their own classes, newcomers, or prospects. Teachers can take some practical steps to be more effective evangelists.

Teachers need to see themselves, not just as communicators of God's truth, but as witnesses to His saving grace. Every believer is responsible to do all in his or her power to reach the lost. Accepting that task is a crucial first step.

Teachers should prepare themselves to lead others to Christ. Developing a consistent pattern of prayer, asking God for opportunities to present the gospel, and seeking His divine wisdom and guidance are critical. Leading someone to Christ is a spiritual victory, a battle that must be won on our knees before it can be won in another's heart. Teachers should also learn to communicate the plan of salvation in a way consistent with the needs and development of their learners. Children are very open to the gospel. Indeed, most people who come to Christ come as children. But the plan of salvation must be explained with words they understand and to which they can respond. Teenage and adult nonbelievers present much the same challenge. They are often unfamiliar with the religious jargon used in the church, so using easily understood language demands careful preparation.

The teacher should set several personal outreach goals.

1. Consistently contact every absent member and prospect with the purpose of seeing nonbelievers come to Christ and become active in the life of the church.
2. Personally ask all students if they know Christ as their personal Savior.
3. Make and take time in the class session to invite students to commit and recommit their lives to Christ. The altar call should be a regular feature of the Sunday School class.
4. Keep track of your students. In Jesus' parable the good shepherd not only knew when one of his sheep was missing, but he knew where to go and get it. Sunday School teachers should

also go and get students who stray from the fold. If their teacher doesn't go to find them, who will?

5. Plan events that give your students an opportunity to invite their unsaved family and friends to come to Sunday School.

6. Consistently present the needs of the lost and the responsibility of believers to reach them.

7. Create a personal prayer list of unsaved class members, visitors, and prospects. Give your students opportunity to add their unsaved friends and family from their own personal lists. Then pray.

Teachers need to enthusiastically support the outreach efforts of the Sunday School and church. Personal commitment to and involvement in outreach efforts are the Sunday School teacher's responsibility, even when such efforts cause inconvenience. For instance, a teacher may be asked to surrender his or her classroom and move to a less desirable space so the church can better utilize the facility. Or the teacher may lose favorite class members when a new unit is created. Meeting these kinds of issues with grace and a firm resolve to fulfill our Lord's Great Commission is a mark of spiritual maturity.

Sunday School teachers should equip their students for the challenges of evangelism. Helping their students gain skills and insights for evangelism begins with the teacher's example but extends to specific instruction, modeling, and practice. The teacher's aim should be not only to see their students grow in their relationship with Christ, but also to equip them to do His work in the world. Students should be encouraged to identify those in their circle of relationships most likely to respond to the gospel.

Conclusion

When did the church stop believing that Sunday School was a place for unsaved people to hear the claims of Christ and commit their lives to Him?

I don't know. But it's too bad we did.

When many churches are stagnant or in decline, harnessing the resources of the Sunday School for evangelism and assimilation really is "awakening the sleeping giant." Make no mistake: This giant really is asleep, and it will take more than a gentle nudge to wake him and send him charging into battle. But it can be done.

No congregation, regardless of size, will survive if it does not reach new people, see them become an active part of that body of believers, and help them grow into fully devoted followers of Christ. Some will just die more quickly than others.

Epilogue

She was a little girl from the wrong side of the tracks. Trapped in the poverty of the Great Depression, her family struggled to survive. Her father was a binge alcoholic with a severe speech impediment. He blamed God for the misery of his life. But he was also an honest, hard-working family man who had overcome incredible obstacles in his own life.

When the little girl was three, neighbors stopped by and asked if they could take her to Sunday School. Every week for the next two years the neighbors stopped by and took the girl with them. When she was five, her family moved and she had no way to get to Sunday School. But when she was eight, her family moved within a mile of the church, and she began to walk to Sunday School. Sometimes when it rained or snowed, families on their way to church would give her a ride. Sometimes they didn't. But she always went.

In a Sunday School class at that little country church, a Sunday School teacher led her to Christ. Another teacher became a sort of foster mother and taught her how to be a Christian woman, wife, and mother. She was the first of her family to graduate from high school and the first to go to college. She married a Christian man and raised five children. All of them are Christians. Two of them are in full-time Christian ministry. All of her grandchildren are Christians, and two of them are in full-time ministry.

One hot summer night when her father was more than seventy years old, she watched him cross the lawn that separated their two houses. He came onto the front porch in his bibbed overalls, work boots, and a sweat-stained straw hat. "Hi, Dad," she greeted him. He stood in the doorway big and gray and old staring at the floor. Finally, he looked up. "Madelyn," he said, "I want you to tell me about this Jesus that Graham preacher talks about." It seems he had been watching a Billy Graham crusade on television that night. She led him to Christ as her teenage son watched from the living room doorway.

When the old man lay dying almost twenty years later, that same boy stood by his hospital bed. They talked as the old man gripped his hand. Now a pastor, her son had stood next to sick and dying people and their families many times. But he had never waited for death with someone he loved. "Are you okay, Grandpa?" he asked.

"Yeah, I know where I'm going. Pray for my boys."

That was his grandfather's last request. He died less than an hour later knowing where he was going and at peace with himself and his God.

It's a true story. I know. I watched my mother lead my grandfather to the Lord that summer night. I'll never forget it. And as he lay dying, I saw the deep peace behind his eyes and was calmed and comforted by the confidence in his voice. You see, I am a debtor to a Sunday School teacher named Edward Kimball, whose ministry cascaded through time to "that Graham preacher" and my grandfather's salvation. I am a debtor to an anonymous Sunday School teacher who picked up a little waif whose father was the town drunk and brought her to Sunday School. I am a debtor to a Sunday School teacher named Edie Robinson, a tiny woman who took my mom into her life and home and taught her what it meant

105

to be a Christian woman, wife, and mother. I am a debtor to my parents who raised me and my brother and sisters in Sunday School. I am a debtor to all those great teachers who put up with me, taught me, loved me and gave me my life and ministry.

The last thing on my grandfather's mind before he died was the eternal destiny of his "boys." My mother had six brothers and two sisters. At the time of my grandfather's death, five of his sons were living and none of them were believers. No Sunday School teacher touched their lives. Nobody reached out to them. They grew up to be honorable, hard-working men like their father but without God. Where was their "Edward Kimball"?

I'm still praying for my grandfather's boys.

Endnotes

[1]"Who led Billy Graham to Christ and was it part of a chain of conversions going back to Dwight L. Moody?", www.wheaton.edu/bgc/archives/faq/13.htm

[2]Thom S. Rainer, *Surprising Insights from the Unchurched and Proven Ways to Reach Them* (Grand Rapids, Mich.: Zondervan Publishing Company, 2001), 47.

The Sunday School Teacher: Body Builder and Bridge

The Tree

He couldn't believe it. Of all the trees and all the days, it had to be this tree and today.

It was summer camp, and fifty soaked and shivering little girls stood huddled on the beach waiting for the next activity. Fifty rowdy boys pushed, shoved, and fidgeted impatiently in the hot sun trying to get to the beach. Right in the middle, the camp manager and maintenance crew were cutting down a tree. There was no safe way to get the girls off the beach or the boys onto the beach.

Men with chainsaws had already climbed the tree and were busily dismembering it. He shouted over the roar of the chainsaws and finally got the maintenance crew to stop. "Hey, Tom, do you have to cut that tree down now? I've got kids at the beach."

The crew in the branches overhead found comfortable spots to sit, and the crew on the ground took a break while he got the girls off the beach and the boys headed in another direction. It was then that he noticed the tree. It was big, in full leaf, and looked perfectly healthy. The trunk was so thick he couldn't wrap his arms around it. As far as he could see, there was no reason to cut it down.

"Why are you cutting down that tree?" he asked.

"Well, if we don't, the next time there's a storm that tree is going to end up in that guy's living room," Tom answered pointing to a nearby summer cottage.

"You're kidding! Doesn't look like there's anything wrong with that tree."

"Carpenter ants. They ate the inside. Has to come down." Tom was usually terse, even more so when he felt challenged.

The man stepped back and watched. The crew in the tree jerked the starter cords, and their saws roared to life. When they finished cutting away limbs, they tied ropes to the tree with the help of those on the ground. When everything was ready, Tom's chainsaw bit into the tree's trunk. The crew leaned on the ropes at just the right moment, and the trunk twisted, cracked, and then broke as the tree crashed to the ground with a hollow thud. When the tree hit the ground, the trunk split open. The core of the tree had been completely eaten away. Nothing was left but sawdust, a bark-covered ring about two inches thick, and hundreds of scurrying carpenter ants. All the hardwood and all the strength of the tree were gone.

"See . . . carpenter ants . . . had to come down . . . no way to save it," said Tom with a self-satisfied smile as he walked away. He tossed the chainsaw into the bed of the camp's pickup truck and headed back to his office.

The crew began cleaning up the remains of the tree. The chainsaws roared, the wood chipper growled, and the crew laughed and talked. As sawdust, the smell of wood, and chainsaw exhaust filled the air, he stood over the hollow corpse and wondered how a tree that looked so healthy and strong could be so damaged and weak.

The answer is in the nature of the tree. The sap, the lifeblood of the tree, moves from roots to branches and back in a porous space between the bark and the hardwood. Each year that porous space is transformed into hardwood, creating a ring, and a new porous space grows. But the strength of the tree is the hardwood at the tree's core, not the sap. This tree had been slowly dying from the inside out. Long before there was any evidence the tree was in trouble, its strength was gone. It couldn't have withstood even a mild storm even though it looked healthy and strong.

As the man gazed at the fractured trunk and poked at the sawdust with his toe, it occurred to him that some churches and Christians are a lot like this tree. They look good on the outside but are hollow at the core.

True Strength

Sadly, some churches that look healthy and strong are in reality damaged and weak. From the outside they give evidence of health and vitality. Their buildings are clean and in good repair. Their worship is vital and alive. Their preacher can preach. The greeters' smiles are genuine and their handshakes firm. Members seem to like and truly care about one another. Activities for children, teens, and adults crowd the calendar. They support missions and proudly display pictures of their missionary families around a map of the world with thin ribbons running from the pictures to their mission field. They pay their bills, support the denomination, and have a good reputation in the community. They even have a trophy case full of plaques, framed certificates, and softball trophies where the glories of the past are enshrined for all to see.

But things aren't always what they seem, even in a church.

Authentic strength is the dream and goal of every church and every church leader. But this doesn't just happen. The apostle Paul gives some insight into how the church becomes strong. He says that the church isn't so much an organization as it is an organism—

like a tree. Paul uses the image of the church as a living body made up of many different parts with Christ as its head.

> The body is a unit, though it is made up of many parts; and though all its parts are many, they form one body. So it is with Christ. For we were all baptized by one Spirit into one body . . . But in fact God has arranged the parts in the body, every one of them, just as he wanted them to be (1 Corinthians 12:12,13, 18).

> And he [Christ] is the head of the body, the church; he is the beginning and the firstborn from among the dead, so that in everything he might have the supremacy (Colossians 1:18).

> Instead, speaking the truth in love, we will in all things grow up into him who is the Head, that is, Christ. From him the whole body, joined and held together by every supporting ligament, grows and builds itself up in love, as each part does its work (Ephesians 4:15,16).

Like the human body, the church is a complex system made up of interdependent, interconnected, yet individual parts. First Corinthians 12 describes the nature of the church.

1. The church is diverse. It is made up of many different kinds of people who have many different functions in the Body.
2. God has gifted members of the Body differently so they can fulfill their function. In this sovereign act of grace, God gives individuals the gifts He chooses.
3. God arranges individuals and their gifts in the Body as He wills, for His purpose is the healthy function and growth of the Body.
4. Members are supposed to function as a unit with each supplying and supporting the rest of the Body's needs.
5. God's gifts are given to individuals "for the common good." They are for corporate edification, not private exaltation.
6. No individual or single ministry is more important than any other. Although some ministries may be more prominent and receive more attention than others, all are equally significant.
7. Christ is the head of all. Each must willingly act in the interest

of the whole and sacrifice for, submit to, support, and supply the rest of the Body as an act of obedience to Christ.

The standard of unity, mutual submission, and support is ministry's highest hurdle. In a healthy and effective church, individual members and ministries act, not in their own perceived self-interest, but in the interest of all. They submit their desires to the greater good. They don't insist on having it their way but on making sure God has His way in their lives and church. That is what Paul instructed in his letter to the Philippians: "Each of you should look not only to your own interests, but also to the interests of others" (2:4).

A local church cannot fulfill its God-given potential or purposes if the members of that body refuse to function as Paul describes. It is possible to a have what appears to be a large and financially successfully congregation without such unity. But the three "b's" (buildings, budgets, and bodies) aren't an adequate measure of effective ministry. A truly successful church meets the test of unity.

Paul included discord in his list of "acts of the sinful nature" (Galatians 5:19–21). Rivalry between believers and ministries isn't God's plan. It doesn't help the church grow and prosper. Moreover, it doesn't bring glory to God or build His kingdom.

Unity in mission, vision, purpose, and ministry is a tough standard for which few strive and even fewer attain. But it is the source of strength in the church.

Building Strength in the Body

The strength and unity of the Body are built through evangelism and assimilation, vision and purpose, ministry and service.

Building the Body Through Evangelism and Assimilation

Effectively connecting the church to the community builds the Body numerically. As the gospel message pours out of a church across its bridges into the community, people who are reached cross over those same bridges into the life and ministry of the church. Establishing this two-way traffic is the only way a church can truly impact its world and add new believers to its ranks. Those new believers become bridges to their families, friends, and neighbors, and the gospel message goes where it never could have gone before.

But that's not all these newcomers do for the church. They also bring their treasure, their financial support for the ministries of the church. They enrich the life of the church with their talents, gifts, and abilities. Finally, they bring their time. Ultimately these newcomers will take their place beside the "old timers" and give themselves in service to the cause of Christ.

Building the Body Through Vision and Purpose

The Body is strengthened and united in faith, knowledge, and love as leadership shares God-given gifts and vision. When believers understand and embrace the same vision and purpose, their energy, creativity, and resources can be focused on accomplishing the same goal.

Shared purpose and destiny welds believers to one another. In times of trial or persecution, vision and purpose energize the church and help believers face difficult challenges. When internal strife and discord threaten the church's unity, this sense of vision and purpose helps believers rise above their differences and get on with reaching a lost and dying world. Shared vision and purpose produce a fierce loyalty among believers and their leaders. Finally, shared vision and purpose create a shared identity that transforms "me" into "us" in the church.

Building the Body Through Effective Ministry and Service

Effective ministry that serves the needs of the Body and its members adds to the strength of the entire church body by helping believers grow in their commitment to Christ. Ministry helps believers overcome struggles and meet the challenges of the Christian life, making the church healthier. Meaningful ministry and service also must reach outside the walls of the church and into the lives of the lost.

Believers find their true purpose in meaningful ministry and service to Christ and to others. All believers are gifted and called to ministry, but those who refuse to answer that call never find the fulfillment it brings. The call to willing, joyful service is at the heart of the gospel and is the only true measure of spiritual greatness. In our service to God, we find spiritual strength. In our service to one another, the bonds of love and loyalty are cemented. And in our service to the world, the hearts and ears of nonbelievers open to the gospel message.

Christlike service does not demand recognition or accolades but never misses the opportunity to recognize and appreciate the service of others. It gives freely without regard to whether it will be repaid. This service doesn't keep score. It is not interested in how much or how many but only in how it can do more and better. It flows generously from hearts of gratitude in those who have freely received the riches of Christ and owe a debt they can never repay. It is gentle, never condescending or controlling. It never makes people feel put down but always lifted up. It is service unlike anything the world knows, because it flows from the heart of God.

The Essential Elements

Building this kind of strength requires two key elements.

Infrastructure

Infrastructure is the collection of components needed to do anything. For example, moving crops from the field to the produce aisle and ultimately to the tables of consumers takes infrastructure. Once harvested, a tomato must be transported to the processing plant where it is inspected, washed, and packaged for sale. Then it

113

must be transported to the store and placed on the shelf so shoppers can squeeze it, smell it, and buy it. Finally, it must be transported to the consumer's home to be placed in a refrigerator until it ends up as part of a dinner salad.

The person who picked the tomato in the field, the truck that took it to the processing plant, the road and bridges the truck traveled on, the processing plant and its employees, the company that made the Styrofoam tray and plastic wrap for the package, the grocery store, the display case, the shopping cart, the car the shopper drove home in, the refrigerator, etc., etc.—it's all infrastructure.

Every church needs infrastructure to be effective. Infrastructure is the myriad of people and processes required to carry out any function. Consider the infrastructure involved in the "welcome" experience of a person's first visit to the church. Here are some of the elements: clear directions to the church, reserved spaces for visitors in the parking lot, friendly greeters at the door, helpful ushers, the church bulletin and welcome packet, the visitor registration process and the person who contacts the visitor. It's all infrastructure and it is essential.

Bridges

Bridges make what would be impossible or very difficult possible and even easy. People, goods, and ideas flow across bridges. Literally, bridges span bodies of water or deep chasms. Figuratively, they span unseen barriers that keep people apart. A bridge can join disparate peoples and communities and foster a sense of unity and common destiny. Without bridges people can't know one another, establish relationships, develop a common identity, or work together for the common good.

Churches need to build different kinds of bridges. A bridge *between the church and the outside community* must be built, or the message of the gospel doesn't get out and people seeking a new life in Christ can't get in. Ministries that create such bridges are essential to the growth of the church and indispensable as the church seeks to influence culture and society.

A bridge must be established *between church leaders and their people.* Without such connections leadership cannot communicate mission, vision, and direction, and the people cannot contribute their gifts, talents, insights, and wisdom or express their needs and concerns. Leaders cannot harness the energies and abilities of their people and concentrate them for the good of the kingdom, and the people cannot fulfill God's call to service.

Relational bridges b*etween individual members of the church, to believers in other churches, and to those around the world* are needed. The church cannot be strong if it is just a collection of strangers. Love and loyalty should mark the church, but that can't happen unless believers connect with one another. That can't happen without the bridges that create those opportunities.

Finally, bridges must be built *between church ministries and organizations.* These connections are essential to the health and vitality of the church. They are the ligaments Paul talks about in Ephesians 4:16 by which the Body is "joined and held together" and by which the whole Body "grows and builds itself up in love, as each part does its work." Relational bridges are needed to connect the ministries of the church, because without them believers may never develop the kind of personal relationships that characterize a healthy church. They may have little or no contact with those who are not part of their ministry. Those who are not part of any ministry in the church are even less likely to develop these valuable relationships.

Effective bridges in the church produce many benefits. For example, when churches reap the benefits of coordination and cooperation, unnecessary duplication is eliminated, and ministries stop competing and start helping one another be successful. Events and activities are scheduled and supported so that everybody wins. Shared vision and purpose are other benefits. Camaraderie develops as people in different ministries come to know one another and understand what the others are trying to accomplish. They come to respect and value one another as important members of the same team. The more effective use of resources is another benefit. As different ministries know and understand one another's needs, they make more effective and efficient use of resources and personnel.

Building this kind of infrastructure in the church isn't glamorous work, but it is essential.

The Sunday School: Building Bridges, Building the Body

Bridge building is easier said than done. But Sunday School is an ideal bridge to connect various parts of the life and ministry of the church. Sunday School is the one ministry of the church that can touch every member of the congregation. As such, it is an ideal bridge between church leadership and the people, between the church and the world, between members of the congregation, and between the various ministries of the church. The structure and organization of Sunday School are well suited to the task. Sadly, few churches take full advantage of those capabilities.

The role of the Sunday School in evangelism and building community in the Body was discussed in chapters 2 and 5. Its role in leadership development will be discussed in chapter 8. As we will see in the following pages, the Sunday School can strengthen the life and ministry of the church by serving as a bridge between the various ministries of the church and between their leadership and people.

The Bridge of Appreciation

Churches develop an array of niche ministries to serve specific groups or meet specific needs. A church may sponsor mid-week club programs for children, offer a women's Bible study or men's ministry, and serve single parents, senior adults, teenagers, or other groups. Churches offer divorce recovery workshops, support groups, weight-loss groups, literacy or English classes, and a host of other need-based ministries. Other ministries like the choir, greeters and ushers, altar workers, and nursery workers also provide valuable service to the church.

Generally these ministries are seen as separate and distinct from the Sunday School. But Sunday School leadership should recognize, appreciate, and value all the ministries of the church, because they are part of the same team. Unfortunately, the relationship between Sunday School and other ministries can be characterized by competition, not cooperation; annoyance, not appreciation; and rivalry, not respect.

Sunday School leadership should promote an atmosphere of appreciation and respect for those who serve the church in any ministry. In addition, Sunday School leaders and teachers should take every opportunity to express appreciation to those who serve the cause of Christ. Furthermore, they should encourage Sunday School staff members to recognize the service of others and express appreciation to them. These are all practical ways to build this bridge.

Building infrastructure begins with genuine appreciation.

The Bridge of Cooperation

Church calendars are crowded, church budgets are strained, facilities are limited, and workers are in short supply. Sound familiar?

Growing ministries inevitably strain available resources. In that atmosphere it is easy to view other ministries as competing for the same resources the Sunday School needs to thrive and survive. "I win, you lose" skirmishes can develop quickly, with each ministry looking out for its own needs. These escalate into turf battles where nobody wins and everybody loses.

Sunday School leaders and staff should do all they can to cooperate with other ministries. Their success should be everyone's concern.

117

If they win, the church wins, and so does the cause of Christ. Here's why: Every other ministry of the church has the potential to help Sunday School be more successful. They open the door to new people and potential Sunday School students. Other ministries, like ushers, greeters, and nursery workers directly support the Sunday School.

An attitude that is generous, flexible, and cooperative rather than self-seeking, rigid, and selfish builds a sense of unity, strengthens the church, and makes every ministry more successful.

The Bridge of Coordination

Sunday Schools share facilities, equipment, and staff with other ministries. There are a limited number of Saturdays each year, a limited amount of money, and a limited number of workers. Therefore, coordination between Sunday School and other ministries is necessary to decrease frustration and increase effectiveness.

Scheduling facilities, equipment, and events in ways that help everyone succeed is an important part of building infrastructure. Free of the confusion and frustration, leaders and staff are free to focus on achieving their ministry goals. Coordination requires respect, a spirit of cooperation, and good communication.

Here are a few practical suggestions: Review the calendar and make sure each ministry can schedule its events. Don't monopolize the church van or bus. Create a process to schedule facilities and equipment. Jointly sponsor some events. Meet with other ministry leaders and determine other practical ways to better coordinate the church's ministries.

The Bridge of Communication

Appreciation, cooperation, and coordination all rely on good communication. Sadly, ministry leaders and their staff tend to communicate within their ministry but not with other ministries. But good communication is essential. Without it nobody succeeds.

Failure to accurately and completely communicate in a timely fashion creates trouble in the church. Communication failure leads to misunderstanding and feelings of being neglected, ignored, or not valued enough to be informed or heard. Lack of communication creates confusion and chaos. It is virtually impossible for any group to accomplish anything meaningful without clear and complete communication. As failure to adequately communicate creates alienation, confusion, and mistrust, so quality communication creates unity, coordination, and trust.

Two practical steps can improve communication between ministries. First, plan times for various groups to meet and share their ministry and vision. Those who serve the same people in different ministries and share the same facilities and equipment should have the opportunity to get to know one another. Second, keep the information flowing. Each ministry should communicate its plans, activities, and needs with the other ministries of the church. Visitor, newcomer, and absentee contact information should be shared with those who serve the same people in other ministries.

The Bridge of Support

Nothing builds mutual respect and strengthens the bonds of ministry more than practical help. Sunday School can support other ministries of the church in concrete ways.

Sunday School can provide and make room in its schedule to train workers for other ministries. Sunday morning is the ideal time to train. Participants don't have to worry about baby-sitters or scheduling conflicts. Sunday School teachers should see this training as a logical and needed extension of the Sunday School's purpose.

Simply showing up to help other ministries with their projects and activities builds camaraderie. Why shouldn't Sunday School classes help at the Pinewood Derby or make gifts for the nursing home visitation team to give to the residents?

Willingly sharing facilities, supplies, resources, and equipment is a matter of good stewardship. It is also a matter of developing friendships and of understanding that the Sunday School needs the support of other groups.

Promoting the events, activities, and achievements of other ministries is another way to show support. Celebrating their accomplishments doesn't diminish the Sunday School's accomplishments. Encouraging Sunday School students to participate in other ministries enriches their lives and builds solidarity between ministries.

Finally, Sunday School leaders, teachers, and staff should pray for those serving in other ministries, their needs, and the needs of their participants. Establishing and coordinating a prayer chain or developing a prayer partner system in which those serving the Sunday School pray for those who do not are practical ways to accomplish this goal.

Last Words

It's obvious, isn't it? Cooperation is better than competition. Coordinated ministry is more effective than ministry chaos. Unity and harmony are better than frustration and conflict. Prayer for one another and appreciation are better than angry and disparaging words. Bridges are better than barriers, and building is better than destroying.

We don't build these bridges for ourselves. We build them for others. We build them for those who do not yet know Christ and for all those who will follow us.

The Bridge Builder
by Will Allen Dromgoole

An old man, going a lone highway,
Came at the evening, cold and gray,
To a chasm vast, and deep and wide,
Through which was flowing a sullen tide.

The old man crossed in the twilight dim;
The sullen stream had no fears for him;
But he turned when safe on the other side
And built a bridge to span the tide.

"Old man," said a fellow pilgrim near,
"you are wasting strength with building here;
Your journey will end with the ending day;
You never again must pass this way;
You have crossed the chasm, deep and wide—
Why build you the bridge at the eventide?"

The builder lifted his old gray head:
"Good friend, in the path I have come," he said,
"There followeth after me today
A youth whose feet must pass this way.
This chasm that has been naught to me
To that fair-haired youth may a pitfall be,
He too must cross in the twilight dim;
Good friend, I am building this bridge for him."[1]

The Toledo War and the Biggest "Big Mac"

In 1837 an act of Congress was necessary to end the Toledo War, a longstanding border dispute between Michigan and Ohio. Ohio became a state in 1803, and in 1805 Congress created the Territory of Michigan. For the next thirty years, Michigan and Ohio both claimed 470 square miles of land that included the city of Toledo on Lake Erie. In 1835 Michigan sought statehood, but legislators from Ohio successfully blocked Michigan's admission to the Union until the border dispute was settled. Tempers flared and armed militias formed on both sides of the border. The longstanding cold war almost got hot.

Fortunately, Congress settled the dispute without a shot being fired. Congress refused to grant Michigan statehood until it gave up its claim on Toledo. Michigan's compensation was the Upper Peninsula. Ohio got Toledo.

Michigan considered the Upper Peninsula poor compensation. For more than 120 years, Michigan was one state separated by a forty-mile-long stretch of water. Five miles wide at the narrowest point, the Straits of Mackinac presented a formidable obstacle to government and commerce.

Traveling between Michigan's upper and lower peninsulas was difficult and dangerous. As early as 1884, people were talking about building a bridge across the straits. In 1923 the state established ferry service across the Straits. Then in 1934 a bridge was finally approved. It would take another twenty years to begin construction.

Construction began in 1954 on a suspension bridge between Mackinaw City in the Lower Peninsula and St. Ignace in the Upper Peninsula. The Mackinac Bridge (affectionately referred to as the "Mighty Mac" or the "Big Mac") was completed in 1957 and is a vital link between the upper and lower peninsulas. A five-mile-long ribbon of steel is suspended over the waters of the Straits of Mackinaw, and traveling between Michigan's two peninsulas is easy.

The need for bridges between ministries and people in the church is just as great. The barriers and obstacles sometimes seem just as wide. Let's hope it doesn't take as long to successfully build a bridge to overcome our differences.

Endnotes

[1]Will Allen Dromgoole, *Rare Old Chums* (New York: L. C. Page and Company, 1898).

The Sunday School Teacher: Activist and Agent

World Changers

Ever heard of the Clapham Sect?

They were a remarkable group of prominent Christians who lived in England at the beginning of the nineteenth century. Great revivals led by the Wesley brothers and George Whitefield had swept the British Isles. From this spiritual renewal emerged Methodism and a strong evangelical movement within the Anglican church, as well as the Clapham Sect. These believers were derisively nicknamed the "Clapham Sect" because most of the members belonged to the Anglican parish of Clapham. All were committed Christians, concerned with the social and spiritual issues of the day, including the abolition of slavery in the British Empire, the establishment of Sierra Leone as a haven for freed slaves, the support of missions and Bible distribution, and the creation of Sunday Schools.

They were more than concerned. They were determined to act.

John Venn, rector of the Clapham parish, was the founder of the Church Missionary Society. After a precarious start, the society

123

began a vigorous campaign to establish pioneer works to carry the gospel to unreached people and nations. Noted for its evangelical fervor, missionary zeal, and fervent preaching, the society became the largest missionary organization in the Church of England. Missionaries from the society evangelized and established churches in Africa, the United States, India, New Zealand, and western Asia.

Zachary Macaulay helped establish missionary works in India and China and founded the University of London. He was editor of the *Christian Observer,* which was published on behalf of the Clapham Sect.

Granville Sharp, an attorney, spent most of his adult life working to free slaves. His defense of a black slave named James Somerset led to the "Somerset Decision" of 1772, which declared that "as soon as any slave sets foot upon English territory, he becomes free." The colony for liberated slaves in Sierra Leone was his idea.

Henry Thornton hosted meetings of the Sect in his home. He was instrumental in forming the Sierra Leone Company and treasurer of the Church Missionary Society and the British and Foreign Bible Society. Founded in 1804, the Bible Society has published the Bible in almost every known language. Its aim is "to encourage the wider circulation of the Holy Scriptures without note or comment."

Hannah More, with the help of the Clapham Sect and others, established a chain of Sunday Schools among the neglected miners in western England. In those schools poor children were taught to read and taught the Bible. A prolific writer, More influenced countless others with her highly popular writings on the Christian life, including many books still in print.

William Wilberforce was the founder and most famous member of the Clapham Sect. Elected to Parliament in 1780, he spearheaded the campaign against slavery in the British Empire. He joined forces with Thomas Clarkson and a number of leading Quakers in 1787 and formed the Committee of Twelve to end slavery. As a result of their efforts, slave trade was regulated in 1788.

In 1807 Parliament abolished slave trade in the British Empire, and the great European powers abolished slavery in Vienna in 1815. Wilberforce retired from Parliament in 1825, but his protégé and fellow member of the Clapham Sect, Thomas Buxton, succeeded in getting Parliament to pass a law abolishing slavery in 1833. Wilberforce, who had worked for more than fifty years to end slavery, died just weeks before that goal was achieved. Thirty years later his influence was felt on this side of the Atlantic when Abraham Lincoln's Emancipation Proclamation and an amendment to the Constitution ended slavery in the United States. Wilberforce also helped establish the Church Missionary Society, the British and Foreign Bible Society, and the Society for Bettering the Conditions of the Poor.

The individual achievements of these people are amazing. Taken as a group, their accomplishments are nothing short of miraculous. This small group of committed Christians changed the course of their society, impacted a great empire, and altered the course of history itself. Their missionary zeal helped launch great spiritual awakenings in North America, Asia, and Africa. The Clapham Sect freed millions of enslaved men, women, children, and their descendants. Millions more were freed from the chains of ignorance, poverty, and social injustice. Multitudes were freed from the bonds of sin and death and found Christ as their Savior. All this because of one small band of committed Christians.

An old saying goes, "Some people are so heavenly minded they are of no earthly good." Like much commonly accepted "wisdom," this sentiment couldn't be further from the truth. The truth is that only those who are truly heavenly minded are ever of any real earthly good.

Introduction

One unfortunate consequence of our modern educational system is the separation of knowledge from action. In an academic environment, mastery of content is the most important element. This results in jokes about educated idiots who have been to school but don't have any common sense and can't get along in the real world. The academic environment values the discovery and acquisition of knowledge for its own sake. The practical value of discovery is of little or no consequence.

There is, however, another tradition in education. In the United States the "land grant" college system, established at what is now Michigan State University and other schools across the nation, sought the practical use of knowledge just as much as its discovery and acquisition. From the medieval guild system right through the skilled trades of today, apprentices have sought masters who can help them understand their craft and develop practical and useful ways to use those skills. In trade schools electricians, plumbers, carpenters, computer programmers, welders, cosmetologists, mechanics, and other skilled people are trained to apply theory in useful ways.

The classic professions have long recognized the importance of training that develops practical skills. Future physicians leave medical school with a wealth of knowledge but must complete an internship and perhaps a residency before they are ready to practice. Future attorneys leave the theory of the law school and often clerk for a law firm or judge to gain practical experience before they take the bar exam and begin to practice law.

It's this simple. Every airplane passenger wants to know that the pilot and copilot not only understand the principles of aerodynamics but also have real-life experience flying airplanes. No one wants to trust his or her life to a person who got straight A's in the history and theory of flight but has never held an airplane's controls.

The church has not been immune from this separation of knowledge from hands-on experience. Increasingly the church has settled for an academic approach to biblical instruction. In many churches the Bible is taught like a history course. Students are

126

expected to know and correctly recite names, events, and places in their proper order. Little attention is given to the significance of those events or their value in daily life. Even when the church addresses real-life issues, the approach is often theoretical. The result is learners who know about God but who may have never personally experienced His power and presence. Churches are full of people who have taken volumes of seminar notes about great Christian parenting and marriage principles who aren't good parents and whose marriages are in trouble. Too many believers have been taught effective evangelism strategies, learned all the right answers, and memorized all the key verses, but they haven't a clue how to lead someone to Christ.

The impotence of much of what passes for Christian education results from its overwhelming focus on information and theory. It is knowing without doing. Many believe that knowing the truth is enough whether or not they ever act on that truth.

No wonder so many have decided Sunday School is irrelevant. They come looking for real answers to real problems and hear the same oft-repeated stories about people who lived and died long ago and far away. Many teachers don't even try to move beyond the theoretical into the practical. Those who do often recite recycled theories about practical applications. Learners almost never have a chance to personally apply biblical principles to their real-life concerns, solve problems, or develop strategies to deal with those problems. Most Sunday School teachers are so busy talking about the who and the what of long ago that they never address the why and the how of today.

But is this the kind of education God wants for His people?

A Different Model

On the edge of the Promised Land, the children of Israel listened to Moses recount God's instructions. "When all Israel comes to appear before the Lord your God at the place he will choose, you shall read this law before them in their hearing. Assemble the people—men, women, and children and the aliens living in your towns—so they can listen and learn to fear the Lord your God and follow carefully all the words of this law" (Deuteronomy 31:11,12).

Notice that the emphasis isn't just on hearing the law. Hearing is the necessary first step. But the goal is to develop a relationship with God, "learn to fear the Lord your God," and "follow carefully all the words of this law." God never intended that His people learn His Word as an academic exercise separate from the conduct of their daily lives. The teaching of His Word was always intended to bring His people into a right relationship with Him and to find its expression in every aspect of daily life.

When the gospel writers tell of the calling of the apostles, they echo this perspective.

> He [Jesus] appointed twelve—designating them apostles—that they might be with him and that he might send them out to preach and to have authority to drive out demons (Mark 3:14,15).

> He called his twelve disciples to him and gave them authority to drive out evil spirits and to heal every disease and sickness . . . These twelve Jesus sent out with the following instructions . . . 'Preach this message . . . heal the sick, raise the dead, cleanse those who have leprosy, drive out demons. Freely you have received, freely give' (Matthew 10:1,5,7,8).

Like believers today, the Twelve were called to be Jesus' disciples, to be learners. Like us, they were called to be with Him and develop a healthy spiritual relationship. Like us, they were called so that they could be sent into the world to carry out His will and work.

But doing is not the automatic result of hearing His Word. Learning by doing prepared the apostles to lead the Church and change the world. In training the Twelve, Jesus didn't just teach them the principles of the Kingdom with His stories, parables, and sermons. Nor was it enough for them to simply be with Him. He didn't expect them to absorb what they needed by spiritual osmosis.

No, Jesus added real-life experiences to His instruction and relationship as a means of spiritual and ministry development.

Many seem to think that hearing the Word and being with Christ in worship is all they need. Our faith was never intended to be the mere acceptance of theological principles and the ability to grasp the breadth and scope of Scripture and church dogma. Christians have always been intended to express Christ's teachings in their daily lives and to change the world through their words and deeds. James admonished: "Do not merely listen to the word, and so deceive yourselves. Do what it says. Anyone who listens to the word but does not do what it says is like a man who looks at his face in a mirror and, after looking at himself, goes away and immediately forgets what he looks like" (James 1:22–24).

Nor was spiritual vitality ever intended to be distinct from the believer's daily life. Spiritual vitality should energize and enable Christian action in the world. The Church was not given the Holy Spirit just to *enjoy* His presence, but to *employ* His power in the ministry of reconciling the world to God through Christ. Jesus said, "You will receive power when the Holy Spirit comes on you; and you will be my witnesses in Jerusalem, and in all Judea and Samaria, and to the ends of the earth" (Acts 1:8).

This truth is clearly demonstrated in the selection of the first seven deacons recorded in Acts 6. Church leaders were looking for people to carry out a mundane real-world task so they could spend more time in "prayer and ministry of the word" (Acts 6:4). The job of waiting on tables and caring for widows isn't what many think of as a high spiritual calling. But look at the job qualifications Peter outlined: "Brothers, choose seven men from among you who are known to be full of the Spirit and wisdom. We will turn this responsibility over to them" (Acts 6:3).

Theirs was a practical ministry fueled by spiritual vitality. The accounts of the ministry of two of these men, Stephen and Philip, demonstrate that these were spiritual giants who did not view their practical service of "waiting tables" as beneath them.

In his epistle, James pointed to the same principle.

> What good is it, my brothers, if a man claims to have faith but has no deeds? Can such faith save him? Suppose a brother or sister is without clothes and daily food. If one of you says to him, 'Go, I wish you well; keep warm and well fed,' but does nothing about his physical needs, what good is it? In the same way, faith by itself, if it is not accompanied by action, is dead. But someone will say, 'You have faith; I have deeds.' Show me your faith without deeds, and I will show you my faith by what I do. You believe that there is one God. Good! Even the demons believe that—and shudder (James 2:14–19).

Truly effective Christian education isn't academic. Effective Christian education rests solidly on sound doctrine, is energized by the Holy Spirit, and emphasizes learning by doing and doing what one learns. The learner is an active participant in the process of exploring, discovering, applying, and using biblical knowledge. That kind of learning requires a teacher who is an effective role model, mentor, guide, partner, and servant, not a superior master or guru.

Sunday School can and should be a place of active learning that results in Christian action in the world and that is an agent of dynamic spiritual life.

Action, Reaction, and Catalyst

The dynamic relationship between learning, action, and spiritual vitality is critical to successful Christian education. Believers, challenged to use what they have learned, put their new biblical insights into practice. Sometimes the results are great. Sometimes the believer walks away from the experience feeling like a failure. Most of the time, attempting to live the claims of Christ is good in some ways, bad in some, and, as far as the believer can tell, meaningless in others.

But from the Christian educator's perspective, there are always three results. First, whether believers judge an action as a success or failure, the experience always reveals great truth. Believers learn things about themselves and about God and gain insights they never could have had without the experience.

Second, while these experiences add to believers' understanding, they also open the door to more questions and issues. Having crossed one threshold, they are ushered into a new dimension of God's work in their lives and in the world. Those new questions push learners into a search for answers and a greater understanding of God and His ways. The challenges of Christian living fuel the need for an even greater measure of God's wisdom, presence, and power. That need sends them back to their teachers and other believers with questions to explore. The cycle continues in an ever-upward spiral of spiritual growth.

Third, these experiences impact believers' spiritual lives. Plainly demonstrated are their weakness and their need for the power and presence of God. This encourages them to seek a more vital relationship with God. It also teaches them that God is their "ever present help" in times of trouble and that they can depend on His strength in their weakness. That knowledge emboldens believers to take on even greater challenges.

If the process works as it should, believers grow in their understanding of God, His will, and themselves. They grow in grace, become more mature disciples, and are better prepared to take on the next set of challenges. They inevitably will face another challenge and be called on to carry out God's will in their lives. And the process begins again.

Active participation in the life and ministry of the church becomes a catalyst for greater learning and spiritual growth. Believers are transformed from passive recipients soaking up greater quantities of biblical information into active participants putting their learning to good use in their lives, in the church, and in the world.

Changing Direction

But how can Sunday School become this kind of dynamic learning environment? If the church is to abandon the failed model of the Sunday School that is satisfied with "religious instruction" and move to a model of active learning, several things have to change. Our vision, our structures, and the roles of teachers, learners, and leaders must be rethought and redefined.

Vision

A North American man and a Bolivian man named Jorge laid ceramic blocks next to each other as they raised the walls of a new church in Santa Cruz de la Sierra, Bolivia. Neither spoke the other's language. Both were trying to learn. The American noticed that the section of wall he was building and the section Jorge was building weren't lining up. The difference wasn't great but would be noticeable. In the little bit of broken Spanish he'd picked up while in Bolivia, the American tried to point out the problem. But he didn't exactly speak Spanish. He spoke what he called "important Spanish": *taco, enchilada, burrito, sopa, salada, café con leche,* and so on.

All he got from his Bolivian friend was a quizzical look. He continued to point, gesture, and explain in mangled Spanish. Suddenly the lights went on; Jorge got it. He responded with a big amused grin, *"No importa, esta bien."* The American understood the grin and he understood that phrase. He had heard it a thousand times since he had stepped off the plane. "It's not important. It's okay." Of course Jorge was right. The wall would be plastered inside and out, and no one would ever see the slight discrepancy in the mud joints.

Unfortunately, many evaluate their Sunday Schools the same way. Regardless of what it does or how it does it, the leaders have the same attitude: "It's not important. It's okay." Unlike Jorge, they are wrong. It is important, it does matter and it's not okay. Accurately taking the measure of the Sunday School begins with a clear vision of what it ought to be and do. It's more important to do the right thing than to do the wrong thing the right way.

The *vision* of the Sunday School must change. No longer can the Sunday School be a place that just delivers biblical and doctrinal information. It must be a place where biblical and doctrinal truth are discovered, explored, and applied by the learners. Learners must examine the significance and meaning of that truth in the church, their lives, and ministries. No students should leave a Sunday School class without coming to grips with the demands inherent in what they discover in God's Word. No students should leave without examining the ways in which God's Word impacts their lives, determining what actions they should take, and feeling moved to act on those demands. Finally, no students should leave a Sunday School class without having had the opportunity to share what they learned as they lived out the truths of Scripture.

This vision for instruction is based on three key beliefs. First, God's Word is always relevant to the believer's life and ministry. Sadly, sometimes teachers and preachers present eternal truth in ways that make it seem irrelevant.

Second, if learners are given the opportunity to explore God's Word for themselves and allowed to discover its truth, they are more likely to respond and act on that truth. Secondhand experiences, whether those of biblical characters, historical figures, or the teacher, lack the power of a personal firsthand encounter with God's Word.

Third, teachers can depend on the Holy Spirit to challenge, convict, and illuminate their learners in ways most meaningful to the learner. Teachers can and should rely on the power, presence, and gifts of the Holy Spirit. But teachers must always remember that the Holy Spirit is at work in the lives of their students as well. The Holy Spirit is more than capable of revealing the truth of Scripture, convicting learners, and motivating them to action.

Laboratory of the Holy Spirit

Once the vision of Sunday School is transformed, the Sunday School must become a "laboratory" of the Holy Spirit. Rather than listening to someone talk about God, learners should be given the opportunity to experience God. Real Christian education cannot happen without the power and presence of the Holy Spirit in the classroom. Religious instruction can happen without the Holy Spirit, but Christian education cannot. This perspective demands that teachers and learners alike come to class having prayed for God's power and presence. It challenges the teacher to lead the class in times of prayer and intercession. It encourages the exercise of the gifts of the Spirit in the class and above all looks to the Holy Spirit to reveal truth.

Christian Action

The Sunday School also should become a platform for Christian action. As a group of believers, the class should find appropriate ways to express the truths they are learning. Teachers need to encourage students to road test the truths they discover. Then the actions they take will become part of the learning process. The kinds of action vary with students' ages, abilities, and opportunities.

In summary, the Sunday School class should be transformed

- from a place where teachers are active and students are passive to a place where students are active participants in their own learning;
- from a place where the Holy Spirit is recognized and discussed to a place where the power and presence of the Holy Spirit are active and integral parts of the teaching/learning process;
- from a place where Christian behavior is discussed and encouraged to a place where students are challenged and given the opportunity to act on their learning in real and practical ways that reflect true Christian character and bring glory to God.

Structures

Implementing practical hands-on learning in the Sunday School is impossible without rethinking Sunday School structures. Most existing Sunday School structures are ideally suited to active learning. The age-graded small group allows personal attention to learners' needs and interests. It can encourage discovery and application at a level and in a way best suited for a specific group of learners. Furthermore, teachers can encourage actions that are appropriate to the age and developmental stage of the learners. Because the Sunday School class is a small and intimate group, trust can develop between the teacher and learners and between learners. Trust encourages self-examination, self-reflection, and appropriate guidance from the teacher.

Fine curricula and teaching resources are available to teachers. Teachers and leaders should select material that encourages first-hand interaction with the Bible and uses age-appropriate teaching methodologies that are relevant to the truth being taught and engage students in meaningful ways. The material should guide the teacher and learner to discover the truth, examine its meaning, and explore ways students can express that truth in their daily lives.

This kind of learning enhances fellowship between teachers and learners as they work together to discover God's truth and as they pray with and for one another. As teachers and learners come to know and care more about one another, they are more likely to trust, support, share with, and act in concert with one another.

One structural barrier many Sunday Schools face is a lack of time. Many churches have expanded the time for corporate worship, and that time has been taken largely from the Sunday School hour. It is possible to tell a Bible story, pop in a video, or lecture about a biblical principle in the abbreviated time slots that pass for Sunday School in many places. But it certainly is not possible for teachers to guide their students to explore God's Word, discover biblical truth, and examine ways it applies to life and ministry in such a short time.

Leaders who don't recognize the value of adequate learning time insure that their Christian education ministries will be irrelevant and ineffective. Church leaders have the obligation and right to use the time they have in ways they see fit. But pirating precious minutes from Sunday School is not the best way to achieve a healthy, thriving congregation or discipling ministry.

The lack of training in most churches and Sunday Schools is another structural obstacle. Too many recruit and place teachers with little or no preparation for their important responsibilities. People taught as passive recipients of someone else's learning will be unlikely to implement active learning in their classrooms no matter how good the curriculum or how much they are encouraged by leadership to teach differently. The only solution is consistent preministry and in-ministry training to help teachers value active learning, provide the skills needed for success, and allow them to experience this kind of learning firsthand. Leadership that fails to train trains people to fail.

The Teacher's Role

The vision of the Sunday School teacher as mentor, guide, and friend is the ideal model for the Sunday School as a laboratory of the Holy Spirit and as a platform for Christian action. In this approach, the teacher's role undergoes several changes.

First, the teacher's role shifts from teller to guide. Because their study, life experience, and maturity are valuable resources in the classroom, teachers never will and never should totally eliminate their role as "teller." But the focus shifts from teachers telling students what they discovered in their study to helping students discover biblical truth for themselves. Skilled teachers use active learning methods that help learners in their search for the truth. Wise teachers help students stay on track and assist them in the discovery process by helping them overcome obstacles and providing resources and direction. Like any good guide, the teacher knows and clearly marks the trail students should follow.

The teacher's role shifts from question answerer to question asker. To help learners discover the truth, teachers should ask questions that lead to greater discoveries. To help learners apply this truth to their own lives, teachers should ask questions that encourage serious reflection. The best way to motivate learners to act on the truth they discover is to ask what they intend to do with their new knowledge.

The teacher's role shifts from talker to active listener. Students who explore, discover, understand, and seek to apply biblical truths have questions and want to share insights. Listening well is an important skill for many reasons. Wise teachers understand that when learners talk about truth they have discovered it becomes ingrained in their lives and memories. People retain far more of what they say than what they hear others say. Wise teachers know that sometimes students misunderstand or draw inappropriate or incorrect conclusions. When students talk, the teacher has an opportunity to help them reflect on their insights, suggest other ways to see an issue or concept, and, if needed, correct the error.

The teacher's role shifts from filling the time to managing the clock. In almost every sport, clock management means victory or defeat. Using class time effectively and helping a group of learners stay on track are vital skills, because Sunday School learners are no less likely than anyone else to be distracted or go off on a tangent. Wise teachers aren't controlled by the clock; instead, they manage the clock.

The teacher's role shifts from being the resource to providing resources. Wise teachers understand that discovering truth is a process that requires many different kinds of resources. They make sure everything students need to discover, explore, understand, and apply God's truth is readily available. The best teaching methodologies and lesson plans fail if necessary pieces are missing.

The teacher's role shifts from focusing on the lesson to focusing on the learner. The needs of learners must take precedence over covering a certain amount of material. Wise teachers understand that different students learn differently and at different paces. Focusing on student needs and abilities helps the teacher make learning challenging but not overwhelming.

The teacher's role shifts from focusing on what happens inside the classroom to what happens outside the classroom. This happens in two ways. First, teachers make sure that students leave the classroom with a clear understanding of practical ways they can apply God's truth in their lives. If that goal is not accomplished, both teacher and students have failed. Second, they make sure that no class begins without the students having an opportunity to reflect on what they are learning as they live the Christian life. Teachers intentionally plan activities outside the class that challenge the class to act on the truths learned. Since various curricula are often built around themes, teachers should plan at least one such event directly related to that theme.

Finally, the teacher's role shifts from talking about God to helping learners experience God. Planning significant times of prayer for needs expressed by the learners and for one another is one way to accomplish this goal. Taking time for testimonies that encourage learners to share their experiences with God is another. Encouraging and inviting the exercise of the gifts of the Holy Spirit within the class is a third way. Altar calls give students opportunity to respond to God and to what they have discovered and give teachers the opportunity to pray with them and for their students.

Conclusion

The Clapham Sect helped change their world and ours. But their great achievements weren't accomplished because they listened intently to great preaching and teaching alone. They discovered the demands of the gospel, developed dynamic lives full of the Holy Spirit, found ways to address the needs of their time and society, and went to work.

There is no way to predict what a church, a Sunday School class, or individual believers could accomplish in their communities and the world if they truly acted on God's truth. Sunday School has the opportunity to challenge believers to greatness—if it will leave behind the failed notion that Christian education is just about communicating biblical and doctrinal information and take up the challenge of preparing Christians for meaningful ministry in the world. If it will become an agent of spiritual life and vitality, Sunday School can call its learners to do great things and make a real difference in their world. In so doing the Sunday School can tap into one of the great motivating forces of human life—the desire to be part of something truly greater.

Epilogue

One of the most effective advertisements ever written appeared in a London newspaper in the early 1900s:

"Men wanted for hazardous journey. Small wages, bitter cold, long months of complete darkness, constant danger, safe return doubtful."

Sir Ernest Shackleton, explorer of the South Pole, wrote that advertisement. Regarding the response to the advertisement, Shackleton noted, "It seemed as though all the men in Great Britain were determined to accompany us."[1] Shackleton knew what sociologists today are discovering: People want to be a part of something bigger than themselves. They want to do something that matters. They want to be a part of something daring and great.

There is nothing greater than the cause of Christ and the ministry of the gospel, no bigger challenge and no more daring or rewarding way of life.

Our problem isn't that we have expected too much of our learners and ourselves. It is that we have expected far too little.

Endnotes

[1] William J. Bennett, The Book of Virtues (New York: Simon and Schuster, 1993), 493.

The Sunday School: Equipping for Life, Ministry, and Leadership

Second Fiddle

He was fifty-three years old, balding, and a thoroughly unimpressive career military officer. He lacked the imperial stature and bearing of MacArthur and the flair of Patton. But he was about to make history.

He graduated sixty-first in a class of 164 from the U.S. Military Academy at West Point, New York. He took twenty-five years to move through the ranks from second lieutenant to lieutenant general. During those long years of service, he held a number of posts. He was an assistant executive in the office of the assistant secretary of war, and he was on the staff of several other more prominent officers for more than a decade. It seemed he would always be an assistant helping to make someone else successful. Nevertheless, he faithfully carried out his duties, took advantage of every opportunity, and learned from every man he worked for.

That day he opened the car door and got in. He turned and faced the president of the United States seated in the back. "Well,

Ike," Roosevelt said, "you are going to command Overlord." With that simple statement, Dwight David Eisenhower went from second fiddle to first chair. He would plan and direct "Operation Overlord," the Allied plan to invade Nazi-dominated Europe on the beaches of Normandy, drive across France, defeat Germany, and end World War II.

Eisenhower would go on to be the president of Columbia University, first supreme commander of NATO, and president of the United States from 1952 through 1960.[1]

Eisenhower ultimately eclipsed many of the men he had served. He would command Omar Bradley, who had graduated ahead of him at West Point. Eisenhower, not Douglas MacArthur or George Marshall, would be elected president, though he had been an assistant to both.

Some say leaders are born. Others believe just as fervently that leaders are made. Eisenhower demonstrates that both perspectives are right—and both are wrong. Eisenhower was born with leadership abilities. Those abilities were sharpened through years of training and dedicated service. Without training and service, Eisenhower's gifts may never have developed, but the converse is also true. The training and experience would have been wasted on a man with lesser gifts.

The same question has perplexed the church. Is gifted ministry a matter of nature or nurture? Are those who serve the church born to it? Or is their life and ministry the result of careful training, service, and preparation? Both are right—and both are wrong.

A Diagnosis[2]

Every church needs its people to be involved in and committed to ministry. Without them the church does not achieve its God-given purposes. It cannot reach its community, care for its members or encourage their spiritual development, or provide dynamic corporate worship. If its members do not serve, the body cannot function correctly. It is handicapped and unable to carry out fully its mission in the world.

But few churches have all the workers they need. Most churches seem to barely survive on the "20-80" rule—20 percent of their people do 80 percent of the work.

All believers are gifted by the Holy Spirit and called to ministry. God has placed them in the Body to use their gifts in concert with others and to fulfill God's will and work in the world. Their gifts vary, but all are essential. Not only are believers gifted, they are called to invest their lives in something meaningful and fulfilling. They want their lives to matter. But very few believers find such places of ministry in their local congregation. Often their gifts and ministries find expression outside the church in parachurch organizations or community agencies.

God has gifted and called church leaders "to prepare God's people for works of service, so that the body of Christ may be built up until we all reach unity in the faith and in the knowledge of the Son of God and become mature, attaining to the whole measure of the fullness of Christ" (Ephesians 4:12,13). Helping believers discover, develop, and deploy their spiritual gifts in the cause of Christ isn't optional for church leaders. It is a divine mandate.

Unfortunately, very few churches have an intentional process to help believers discover their gifts, respond to God's call, develop skills needed for success, and find a place to use their gifts to further the cause of Christ in the church and in the world.

If "every-member" ministry is God's will, if every church needs involved and committed people, if every believer is gifted and called to ministry, then why do so few believers find their place of ministry in the church? Why do so many churches limp along without the help they need? And why do so many church leaders invest so little in training workers?

There are many reasons. One is that many pastors and believers *misunderstand their roles,* the nature of the ministry, and their responsibilities to each other. Pastors sometime feel they are called to do the work of the ministry, not prepare others for ministry. Believers sometimes see ministry as something they hire the pastor to do, not something to which God has called them. They view service in the church as something they do "for the pastor," not as an act of obedience to God and His call on their lives.

Church leaders sometimes operate under *false assumptions.* Pastors assume their people don't want to be involved. They're wrong. People want to serve Christ and find meaningful ways to express their gifts and callings. But they don't want to feel forced to do something for which they are not gifted and have not been trained. They do not want to be so weighted down with church work that their families suffer. They want to be treated with respect and appreciation and not feel used.

Church leaders suffer from the *tyranny of the urgent.* Overburdened by their day-to-day responsibilities, pastors are often forced to put off whatever they can. Because training can be put off without creating an immediate crisis, it often is. Sadly, this short-term gain quickly becomes a long-term pain. Because they don't invest time and energy in recruiting and training workers, no one is available, qualified, or prepared to help carry the load. Because there are so few equipped to help, pastors end up carrying more and more of the load. That ever-increasing workload forces them to put off recruiting and training. It's an ugly, self-perpetuating cycle.

Some believers don't get involved because of *fear.* Since there is no process to help them discover their gifts, they fear being asked to do something that isn't meaningful to them. Because there is no process to help them find an appropriate place of ministry, they fear being forced to do something that doesn't fit their gifts and callings. Because there aren't enough workers, they fear being overwhelmed, overburdened, and asked to carry an ever-increasing load. Because there is no consistent recruiting strategy, they fear being stuck forever with no way out. Because there is little or no training to help them succeed, they fear failure.

Many church leaders are also afraid. They are afraid of releasing important ministry to those who may fail or create problems instead of solving them. Afraid of disloyalty and the devastating consequences of entrusting ministry to those who cannot be trusted, they prefer going it alone. They are afraid that the success of others may somehow diminish them. Already stretched to their limit, they fear that growing ministry will mean there is more for them to do.

Many church leaders *don't know how to train.* It's not their fault. No one ever taught them. Instead, they tend to invest their time, effort, and energy in other areas of ministry. It's easier to just do it than to train someone else.

Failing to effectively recruit and train workers has inevitable and predictable results. Because spiritual health and growth require the exercise of ministry, untrained believers never fully develop their spiritual or ministry potential. Churches plateau and never impact their world the way God intended, because there is a limit to how much the pastor and a few others can do. Churches develop the revolving-door syndrome, because failure to involve believers in ministry keeps them from developing friendships and prevents a sense of ownership and responsibility. Ministry is an anchor in the lives of believers.

The low involvement of believers in ministry is not good and is not God's plan. Without an effective recruiting and training strategy, congregations are locked in a cycle of failure.

Prescription

If low involvement is the disease, what is the cure?

Church leaders must make preparing God's people for works of service their first priority and the cornerstone of their ministry.

They must develop and implement effective recruiting and training strategies.

Pre-Recruiting Process

First, the church must recognize and implement *prerequisites for success.*

1. *Establish limited ministry contracts.* Ministry in a local congregation should be limited in two ways—duration and scope. Each person should commit to a ministry for no less than one year. At the end of that commitment, they should have three options. They may opt to continue their current service, assuming they have successfully fulfilled their ministry requirement. Second, they could transfer to another ministry. Third, they could quit. Gracefully releasing people from ministry paves the way for their return, avoids the problems created by burned-out and frustrated workers, and opens the door of ministry to others.

Ministry should also be limited in scope. Believers should focus on one ministry, not three or four. One way is to limit a believer's involvement to one major and one minor ministry. While no ministry is more important than another, some require a major time commitment, and others do not. An easy rule of thumb identifies a major ministry as one that requires involvement other than scheduled service or event time (for example, teaching Sunday School), while a minor ministry is one that requires involvement only during a service or event (for example, ushering or greeting).

The benefits of limited involvement are many. It prevents burnout. It opens the door of ministry to others in the congregation. It improves quality as believers concentrate on a ministry rather than spreading themselves too thin. And it is easier to recruit.

2. *Write clear job descriptions.* Recruiting is much easier when people know what they are getting into. Their performance improves when they know what is expected. They are less frustrated and

146

more likely to stay when they have been given the respect of the truth. Don't minimize. Don't sugarcoat. Challenge them with the great opportunities of ministry.

Job descriptions should include a clear statement of responsibilities, qualifications, and other expectations. These should include a spiritual and doctrinal agreement, clearly articulated lifestyle expectations consistent with the church standards of holiness, and a detailed explanation of what is expected of those who serve in ministry.

3. *Recruit for training, not positions.* Recruiting for a ministry position without determining the person's gifts, providing training, or considering their qualifications is a mistake. All of this can be accomplished as part of an effective training process. People are also more likely to sign up for training than take on any specific ministry. A person who is recruited for a specific ministry may refuse but willingly take on another ministry assignment if he or she is given training and the opportunity.

4. *Develop a church-wide recruiting system.* A bane of church life is the competition between ministries for help. They end up cross-recruiting and asking people already involved in ministry to join their ministry as well. Some are inevitably better recruiters than others, creating riches for some ministries and poverty for others.

All church ministries and their leaders should be involved in the recruiting/training process. Their participation should be part of a concerted effort to help all believers discover, develop, and deploy their gifts in ways that benefit the church and fulfill their gifts and callings.

5. *Adopt a "big circle" approach.* In an effort to protect the church, leaders sometimes create barriers to recruitment. They require newcomers to be part of the body for a specific period of time, to complete a lengthy training process, or to become members of the congregation. While these and other safeguards may be appropriate for placement in ministry, they should not be

barriers to training. All believers should be eligible for a training process that leads to ministry. In that process they can be helped to satisfy the church's requirements for ministry.

6. *Recruit and train consistently.* Recruiting and training for ministry should be a consistent part of the life of the church. Crisis recruiting communicates failure and disorganization, not success and effective ministry. Depending on the size of the congregation, a recruiting/training cycle may be implemented quarterly, biannually, or annually.

It is important that people are recruited and trained before they are needed. This makes it possible for the church to add ministries and new units in an orderly and predictable way. Thoroughly trained new workers are more effective because they haven't been rushed into service.

7. *Set a goal for "every-member" ministry.* The Bible is clear: All believers are gifted and called to ministry and will be held accountable for the stewardship of their ministry gifts. Church leaders are responsible to help prepare believers for ministry. The goal can and should be nothing less than recruiting, training, and placing all qualified members in ministries consistent with their gifts and callings and the needs of the church.

Recruiting Strategy

Church leaders should create and implement an *effective recruiting strategy.* The first five elements of the strategy below should precede participation in preministry training. The second five can be incorporated into that training.

1. *Pray.* Jesus taught us that because "the harvest is plentiful but the workers are few," we should "ask the Lord of the harvest, therefore, to send out workers into his harvest field" (Matthew 9:37,38). Ministry is ultimately a spiritual endeavor, and recruiting for ministry is a spiritual battle that must be won with prayer.

2. *Promote ministries consistently.* The ministries of the church

should be consistently presented to the congregation. Their successes and victories should be celebrated and their vision and purpose clearly stated. Too often the only time church members hear about a ministry is when there is a need or problem. Frequently these alerts come from frustrated lay leaders or pastors overwhelmed with the problems created by a lack of help.

3. *Write job descriptions.* See discussion earlier in this chapter.

4. *Conduct a people search.* Leadership should identify those who are eligible for recruitment. Any believer, not currently involved in ministry, who meets the other qualifications is a candidate for pre-ministry training.

5. *Approve prospects.* Before contacting any potential worker, recruiters should ask their pastor to review and approve the prospects. This safeguard prevents those who are not qualified from serving and avoids disappointing and hurting the feelings of those who believe a door of ministry is open to them when it isn't.

6. *Present the ministry clearly.* Prospects need an opportunity to examine the ministries of the church and to understand the responsibilities, opportunities, and purpose of each.

7. *Allow prospects to observe the ministry.* Prospects should experience the ministry firsthand before they are asked to serve. Leaders should not assume prospects know and understand the ministries of their church. The opportunity to ride a Sunday School bus, sit in a class, join a visitation team, or experience any other ministry is critical to helping believers find a ministry and make a long-term commitment.

8. *Allow time for prayer and thought.* Too often people are rushed into ministry. Encouraging prospects to pray and seriously consider their commitment is in their interest and the church's interest. Workers who join a ministry after serious thought and prayer and who see their ministry as a response to God's call on their lives are more likely to serve long and well.

9. *Call for a decision.* Leaders need to call for a decision and ask

for a commitment. Formalizing workers' decisions with a ministry covenant and/or a commissioning service solidifies their commitment.

10. *Provide training.* Because effective training helps people succeed in ministry, it is critical to successful recruiting. Practical, hands-on, skill-oriented training helps workers be more effective. Success and satisfaction are inextricably linked. Workers who feel they are making a significant contribution are more likely to perform well and serve consistently than those who feel like frustrated failures.

Preministry Training and Placement Strategy

An *effective preministry training and placement strategy* is the next step. This strategy should incorporate the following.

A. Introduction to Ministry

Prospects should spend significant time being introduced to ministry in the local church. Addressing these issues is at the foundation of future effectiveness.

1. Every-Member Ministry
2. Spiritual Gifts
3. The Church and Your Ministry
4. Outreach and Evangelism
5. Qualifications and Responsibilities
6. Ministry Organization and Structure
7. Our Church in Ministry: Overview
8. Our Church in Ministry: Observation
9. Committing to Ministry

These nine topics can be presented as part of a preministry training class over a nine-week period or as part of a seminar. Those who successfully complete this portion of training and are qualified for ministry then have the opportunity to choose an area of ministry consistent with their gifts and calling. The next step isn't placement in ministry but additional training designed to equip them for service in a specific ministry. This training has both in-class and on-the-job components.

B. Ministry Preparation

Once a prospect, in concert with church leaders, has determined an area of ministry for which he or she is qualified, gifted, and called, the church should give specific, practical training. This training will vary in content and format depending on the ministry, its needs, and its requirement. It may or may not take place in the classroom, and it may or may not precede the on-the-job component.

For those anticipating a teaching ministry, the training should include the following.

1. How People Learn
2. A Look at the Learner: Learner Characteristics
3. A Teaching Plan That Works
4. Preparing to Teach: Inside and Outside the Classroom

C. Internship

An essential and overlooked aspect of training is an internship that provides on-the-job training. Some aspects of ministry can be learned only by doing.

This kind of training should provide three distinct experiences.

1. Observation

For two sessions the trainee should simply observe his or her mentor. Ample time should be allowed for the mentor to explain the ins and outs of the ministry and to answer questions and concerns.

2. Partial Participation

After this period of observation, the trainee should be allowed to participate by carrying out certain parts of the ministry while the mentor observes. This participation should escalate over a specific period of time (four sessions) until the trainee takes over. Again, ample time for reflection and interaction with the mentor is critical.

3. Full Participation

The trainee should switch roles with the mentor and do the ministry while the mentor observes (two sessions). Feedback, constructive criticism, and encouragement from the mentor should follow each of these experiences.

Two components are essential for a successful internship. First and most critical is the selection and preparation of the mentor. Those who mentor prospective workers should be the very best at what they do and be able to effectively instruct others. Second, on-the-job training takes time. A minimum of eight weeks or eight experiences should be allowed. Again, it is dangerous to press prospective workers into service before they are fully prepared.

D. Placement

The final step in the recruiting/training process is effective placement. Everything rises and falls on this final step. The following criteria should be met before anyone is placed in a specific ministry.

1. The prospect's gifts and calling match the ministry's needs and requirements.
2. The prospect has met the spiritual, lifestyle, and ministry requirements.
3. The prospect has completed the required training.
4. The prospect has committed to the ministry and to fulfill its requirements.
5. The prospect has demonstrated his or her loyalty, consistency, and servant heart.

Sometimes, despite the fact that everything that can be done has been done, people discover they are not well suited for a specific ministry only after they have been placed. They should not be forced or even encouraged to stay no matter how much they are needed. This only leads to frustration and ultimately failure. Instead, they should be given another opportunity in a ministry more suitable to their gifts and callings. If that doesn't work, they can be placed again and again until they find their position in the Body. It's more important that they ultimately find a place of ministry where they are satisfied and happy than placing them quickly or filling a slot in the church's organizational flow chart.

Proverbial wisdom reminds us that "timing is everything." How long should a prospect be involved in preministry training? If the training stretches on and on, many prospective workers will grow discouraged. If the training is too brief, they won't be adequately prepared for service and may fail. Finding the balance is critical for success. As described, this preministry strategy takes six months from recruitment to placement. That's long enough to provide adequate training and to gauge the faithfulness, qualifications, and abilities of prospective workers and for them to pray and consider God's leading in their lives. But it's not so long that people get discouraged.

Can new workers be taught everything in just six months? Obviously not. The key is to provide quality training so they can start well and then to provide ongoing training to help them sharpen their skills.

E. In-Service Training

No preministry training strategy can give church workers everything they need to succeed. If church leaders are serious about preparing believers for ministry, they must provide ongoing training. This training should encourage several things in the lives of believers and in their ministries.

1. Skill Development

There is always a need to improve the skills required for effective ministry. Without ongoing training opportunities, workers may have no way to grow.

2. Spiritual Development

Ministry is, always has been, and always should be a spiritual endeavor. All too often those serving in ministry are so busy investing in others that they neglect their own spiritual journey.

3. Problem Solving/Conflict Resolution

People who work together inevitably will face problems and disagreements. In-service training gives workers the opportunity to air their concerns and gives leadership the opportunity to solve them. Unresolved problems and disagreements fester and present an ongoing impediment to ministry.

4. Communication, Feedback, and Affirmation

In-service training provides an effective vehicle to keep workers informed, to hear their concerns and suggestions, and to express appreciation and recognize significant achievements.

5. Planning

Much ministry failure and frustration isn't due to lack of skill, dedication, or diligence; it is the result of poor planning and communication. Regular and consistent in-service training can help overcome this barrier to effective ministry.

6. Accountability

Training gives leadership the opportunity to reinforce ministry expectations, motivate workers, provide resources, and hold workers accountable for their performance.

Quality in-service training has other important characteristics. It should be required for all workers as part of their ministry commitment. It should be ministry and age focused so that training can be as practical as possible. It should be a frequent (monthly or quarterly) and consistent part of church life and ministry. Finally, it should be scheduled at times when there are few or no conflicts so that people can attend. These training events can be supplemented with video or audio resources or participation in district or other training events, but they should not be replaced by them.

The Sunday School: Equipping for Life, Ministry, and Leadership

For several reasons, Sunday School is the ideal vehicle to coordinate and provide an effective recruiting and training strategy for the church. First, Sunday School offers the church *a place and time* for preministry training. As mentioned earlier, it is a time when most people are available, so scheduling conflicts can be avoided. Since the church nursery is open and classes are offered for children during the same Sunday School time, parents have no need to arrange for baby-sitting. Furthermore, it saves having another night out away from family and other responsibilities.

The Sunday School offers a *rich recruiting pool.* Adults and older teenagers who regularly participate in Sunday School are likely candidates for other ministry. They have already demonstrated the faithfulness and teachable spirit essential for successful ministry.

Many highly skilled teachers, support staff, and administrators who could serve as *mentors* are already at work in the Sunday School. Their talents and expertise could be tapped to equip those who will teach and lead the Sunday School and other ministries. Because many of the skills they possess are transferable to other ministries, it makes sense to train workers in Sunday School.

Sunday School also has great training *expertise.* After all, teaching and training are at the center of the Sunday School's ministry. Moreover, because Sunday School is the one agency of the church that *spans all age levels,* it can support ministries designed to serve specific ages or groups. Again, this expertise can greatly benefit other ministries in the church.

A whole church recruiting strategy requires *coordination and cooperation.* The Sunday School and its leaders are in an ideal position to serve the church and its ministries. It keeps the most complete records and is in touch with many prospects and potential trainers.

Finally, the Sunday School makes sense because training for ministry is at the heart of its *purpose and vision.* Sunday School can also support in-service training in many of the same ways.

Creating a Coordinated Recruiting/Training Strategy Through the Sunday School

The church and its ministries should *adopt and support a whole church recruiting/training strategy.* Without that commitment the processes cannot work.

Create a task force made up of leaders representing the various ministries of the church to insure cooperation and coordination. It is critical that all those who have a stake in the success of the strategy have a place at the table and a voice in the decision-making process.

Establish leadership. For all the reasons stated above, it makes sense to ask the Sunday School superintendent, Christian Education director, or his or her designee to head up the recruiting/training strategy. Although this may not be the best approach in some situations, identifying leadership and responsibility is the only approach that will work in any situation.

Next, *plan the work and work the plan.* Pray, plan, promote, produce. Those are the keys to success in any endeavor.

Administer the strategy in a way that *benefits all.* If one ministry seems to benefit more than others, people will lose confidence in the strategy. The criteria for recruitment and placement can't be what seems best for one ministry. It must always reflect the gifts and callings of the people and the needs of the church.

Without pastoral *support and involvement,* the strategy cannot succeed. Involving the pastor in every step of the process in essential.

God has blessed the Church with gifted and called people. He has already gifted the Church with all it needs to build the Body and reach the world. But without an intentional and effective way to help people discover, develop, and use their gifts, they can never fulfill God's will for their lives or His purposes for the Church. With training and experience, these same believers can develop powerful ministries and rich spiritual lives.

The tragedy of many churches is that their greatest treasure is never discovered or developed. It is just as tragic for individual believers. They can never become all that God intended and will never perform ministry or find the fulfillment of faithful service. The need is there. The people and gifts are there. But leadership has failed to challenge, motivate, and equip individuals for service.

It can happen in Sunday School.

Epilogue

They said he was an empty suit, that he lacked "gravitas" and wasn't smart enough to do the job. To many he was a thoroughly unimpressive middle-aged man who lacked the personality and charm of his predecessor and the intelligence and seriousness of his opponent. He often stumbled over his own words and seemed ill at ease in public. He lost the popular vote and was elected president by the narrowest of margins in the electoral college. It took a decision by the United States Supreme Court to end the controversy and put him in the White House.

But just days after terrorists destroyed the World Trade Center in New York City on September 11, 2001, George W. Bush walked the ruins shaking hands and thanking the police and firefighters for their courageous service. He climbed on a pile of rubble, and with a bullhorn in one hand and his other arm around the shoulder of a weary firefighter, he addressed the crowd.

Someone in the back of the crowd called out, "We can't hear you, George!"

His impromptu response, "I can hear you, and soon those who brought down these buildings will hear from all of us," spoke of his

157

defiance and determination and brought wild applause from the crowd.

In the eyes of many, George W. Bush suddenly became their president. No longer an empty suit, he became a world leader worthy of their respect while standing in the rubble of the World Trade Center.

In the weeks and months that followed, the question was asked over and over again: Did the tragedy of September 11 suddenly make George W. Bush a real leader and a real president? Some thought so. Others argued that those events just gave the nation the opportunity to see the real man.

Both were right—and both were wrong.

Endnotes

[1] *World Book Encyclopedia,* 1957 ed., s.v. "Eisenhower, Dwight David."

[2] The author revised and adapted the material in this chapter from an earlier chapter he wrote for *Teacher Training Manual* (Ventura, Calif.: GL Publicaitons, 1982), 22–35.

Conclusion

The Great Emancipator, Abraham Lincoln, was a man well acquainted with personal and professional failure.

In 1832 Lincoln lost his job.

That same year he lost his bid for a seat in the Illinois legislature in a humiliating defeat.

Having failed in his bid for public office, he went into business. That business failed in 1833. He spent the next seventeen years paying debts incurred by his unscrupulous partner.

He won a seat in the Illinois legislature in 1834.

He met and fell in love with a beautiful young woman and asked her to marry him. She died in 1835 before they were married.

In 1836 he suffered a nervous breakdown.

He was defeated in his bid for speaker of the Illinois House in 1838.

In 1842 Lincoln married Mary Todd. By all accounts it was a difficult and troubled marriage.

In 1843 he failed to win the nomination of the Republican Party for the U.S. Congress.

Though he was elected to Congress in 1846, he lost his bid for reelection in 1848.

In 1849 he sought but failed to get an appointment to the U.S. Land Office.

He ran for the U.S. Senate in 1854 and was badly defeated.

In 1856 Lincoln was a candidate for the vice presidency and was once again defeated.

The debates with Douglas typified Lincoln's hard-fought run for the Senate in 1858. Douglas became the U.S. senator from Illinois.

Lincoln was elected president of the United States in 1860.

Reelected in 1864, Lincoln was assassinated on April 14, 1865, at Ford's Theater in Washington, D.C., by failed actor and Confederate sympathizer John Wilkes Booth.[1]

Despite his defeats and failures, Abraham Lincoln became one of our nation's greatest heroes. He guided a divided nation through the dark and horrible days of the Civil War and presided over the worst military slaughter in our history. His experience, personal defeats, and professional failures stood him in good stead as one Union general after another was outfoxed, outfought, and out-maneuvered by Confederate military geniuses like Stonewall Jackson and Robert E. Lee.

In the midst of the carnage, Lincoln knew that ordinary measures were not enough. The old ways just weren't good enough. It was in the worst of those dark days that Lincoln wrote, "The dogmas of the quiet past are inadequate to the stormy present. The occasion is piled high with difficulty, and we must rise with the occasion . . . so we must think anew and act anew."[2] And that is exactly what Lincoln did. His armies won the war and his wisdom won the peace. He didn't live to see it, but the nation split by bloody civil war became one again, overcame the hate of its past, and built a brilliant future.

"We must think anew and act anew."

Throughout its long history, the Sunday School has enjoyed

periods of great triumph and prominence in the life of the church. More recently, the Sunday School has fallen from favor in the eyes of many. Some have written its epitaph and declared it irrelevant in a modern society. Many have abandoned the Sunday School as an institution and tried to replace it with other strategies and programs. Some have kept the Sunday School as an institution but sought to augment it with other ministries. Many more have kept the Sunday School out of a sense of loyalty or tradition or because they simply haven't known what else to do, but it has been relegated to second-string behind more glamorous ministries.

Starved of vision, leadership, recruiting, training, and the resources needed to succeed, the Sunday School has slowly but steadily declined in its influence and effectiveness. In its decline some have pointed a finger at the Sunday School and declared smugly, "See, I told you so!" It is the epitome of a self-fulfilling prophecy.

We must think anew.

The Sunday School, as many have perceived it and experienced it, has failed. In too many places, it is not viable and does not serve the church very well. The church has an eternally important job to do, making disciples, and it must find effective ways to get that job done. Before we relegate the Sunday School to the dusty museum of church history, however, we must think anew. This book has been an attempt to cast a different (but certainly not new or unique) vision of the Sunday School, to challenge church leaders, both clergy and lay, to "think anew" about the Sunday School. All of the fundamentals for effective church-wide evangelism, assimilation, instruction, fellowship, and ministry in the community already exist in the Sunday School. But many have never considered its potential. We must think anew and act anew.

Insanity is sometimes defined as thinking we can do the same things the same way and get different results. It is insane to think we can do Sunday School the same old way and get different results. Sunday School isn't a bad idea. It's a great idea badly done. But Sunday Schools will continue to languish if church leaders do not act differently and take full advantage of its capabilities. Many churches, unable to replace the important functions of a well-run Sunday School, will continue their steady downward spiral.

For some congregations, awakening this sleeping giant isn't an option; it's a matter of survival. If they are to survive, they must implement the building blocks of a healthy church. The Sunday School offers a cohesive strategy to do just that. It offers curricula, support, training, and all the pieces of "infrastructure" needed to be successful. Any size congregation can have a successful Sunday School. All it takes is vision, leadership, and hard work.

No other strategy offers the complete package of a carefully structured and skillfully implemented Sunday School. Although many have experimented with different ways to carry out the mission of the Church in the world, most have fallen well short of their goals. Others will continue to experiment, hoping to find a more effective way to win the world and build the Church. A better and more comprehensive strategy may emerge one day. Until then, churches and their leaders will find that an old-fashioned idea, long viewed as inferior and out of step with our world, can be a powerful tool. But we must think anew and act anew.

A Tale of Two Churches

(The story of these two churches is true. Names and details have been altered.)

In 1976 America was emerging from the humiliation of Vietnam, Watergate, and the resignation of Richard Nixon. Gerald Ford, the only American president never elected as either president or vice president, was locked in a fierce election campaign. He would lose to a former Georgia governor and peanut farmer named Jimmy Carter. Great events marked the year. The *Viking 1* and *Viking 2* spacecrafts landed safely on Mars. North and South

Vietnam were reunited after twenty-two years of bitter separation and more than thirty-five years of war becoming the Socialist Republic of Vietnam. The Apple computer company was founded and fired the first shots of the personal computer revolution. Chinese leaders Chou En-lai and Mao Tse-tung died. The Cincinnati Reds beat the New York Yankees in four games and claimed the World Series. Israeli military commandos staged a stunning raid at the airport in Entebbe, Uganda, and rescued one hundred hostages from terrorist skyjackers. African-American author Alex Haley received the Pulitzer prize for literature for his book *Roots: The Saga of an American Family*, a mixture of fact and fiction based on his family ancestry.

That summer, while the world celebrated the Olympic spirit at the summer games in Montreal, America marked the bicentennial of the Declaration of Independence and the American Revolution. All across the nation, communities celebrated in every conceivable way. Boston Harbor, the site of that famous tea party, hosted a parade of tall ships. Americans planted red, white, and blue gardens; sewed quilts; staged concerts and plays; buried time capsules; and created songs, poems, sculptures, and paintings. The streets were lined with flag-waving people watching parades of costumed people and covered wagons. Almost every grassy park was overrun with Revolutionary War reenactors. Americans staged pie-eating contests and wheelbarrow races, hosted old-fashioned picnics, and festooned every possible surface, including railroad locomotives, with red, white, and blue. On the Fourth of July, magnificent fireworks displays filled America's skies, and Americans paused to reflect on and rejoice in their heritage.

It was a time for Americans to focus on the glory of their beginnings and the achievements of the past, put the tragedies of Vietnam and Watergate behind them, and look with hope to a new and bright future. It was a birthday party like no other. In many ways, 1976 echoed Charles Dickens' famous opening to *A*

Tale of Two Cities, "It was the best of times, it was the worst of times."

That year two congregations in the same metropolitan area looked with hope to the future. Both welcomed new pastors with great enthusiasm and expectations. These men took up their duties within a month of each other. And, in a strange coincidence, both left their congregations within a few months of each other thirteen years later.

In some ways these churches and men were very similar. Both churches were of the same denomination. Both congregations would experience tremendous growth during the tenure of these pastors. Both would launch Christian schools. Both would relocate to new facilities. Both men would surround themselves with outstanding pastoral staff and lay leadership. Both leaders and congregations were committed to missions at home and around the world. Both would leave an outstanding legacy for their successors.

In other ways the churches and men were very different. Both men were great leaders, but they had very different leadership and personal styles. Both were great churches, but they had very different histories. Congregation A was one of the fellowship's great historic churches with a long and honored past. While more than twice the size of its younger sister congregation, A was in a slow and steady decline. Congregation B did not have the heritage or history but was a church on the rise. The churches served different kinds of people. The largely white-collar and professional congregation of one was very different from the salt-of-the-earth, hard-working, blue-collar people of the other.

Both churches grew dramatically during each pastor's tenure. But they grew differently. At the end of five years, morning worship attendance at congregation B had more than doubled from 440 in 1976 to 950 in 1980. Growth in the same period at congregation A was not as dramatic (1,100 in 1976 to 1,300 in 1980).

By the end of their tenures in 1989, morning worship at congregation B had exploded and averaged 2,660 while congregation A had grown steadily to 1,802.

As these congregations transitioned to new leadership in 1989, both faced incredible struggles. When the time came, both congregations excitedly welcomed new pastors. In less than two years, both new pastors were forced to leave under a cloud of controversy. Again each church sought and found another pastor. They too were both gone in less than fifteen months. There were extended periods with no pastoral leadership in either church. Experienced and valued members of the pastoral staff, key lay leaders, and influential families drifted away from both. Ultimately, both congregations needed, sought, and received help from their fellowship's state office.

Conflict, controversy, and bitter battles over the style and substance of their new pastor's ministry erupted in both congregations. Each new pastor's vision and leadership seemed at odds with the church's past and the dreams and desires of its lay leaders. Both congregations fractured under the pressure of the struggle for control of the church and its future. Hundreds became religious refugees, seeking and finding safe haven in other congregations.

Finally, both congregations found new long-term leaders. They believed these men would help them overcome their struggles, regain their past prominence, and lead them into a bright future.

Weathering the Storm

The churches faced and weathered their storms very differently. Between 1989 and 1991, morning worship attendance at congregation B dropped by more than 50 percent, and within five years had dropped from its peak of 2,660 to 760. The collapse of the Sunday School was even more dramatic. Congregation B reported at its peak 2,570 in Sunday School. Within four years attendance bottomed out to an average attendance of just 53. In 1993 the Sunday School rebounded slightly, but morning worship continued to decline.

Congregation A also suffered losses. But its losses, in both average Sunday School and morning worship attendance, were measured in the hundreds, not the thousands. From its peak of 1,800 average morning worship attendance in 1989, congregation A dropped to 1,410 three years later. In that same period, Sunday School attendance dropped from an average of 1,450 to 1,280.

Sunday School in the Eye of the Storm

The circumstances leading to the rise and fall of these two churches are a complex web of many different factors. No one factor can account for all that happened, but the important place of Sunday School in this story cannot be overlooked.

Congregation A had a long tradition of high-quality, closely graded, small group–oriented Sunday School complete with an effective recruiting and training strategy. Congregation B did not. In the middle of the transition, Sunday School attendance at congregation A actually rose slightly (from 1,230 in 1990 to 1,280 in 1991). When the storms came, Sunday School, with its network of relationships, mature lay leaders, and strong sense of community and mission, stood firm.

Congregation B reported much larger Sunday School attendance during its rise and dropped much faster and further. A look behind the numbers reveals that congregation B never developed the same kind of strong discipling ministry that characterized the Sunday School in congregation A. Explosive growth, multiple services, and inadequate facilities made it impossible. Alternatives were tried with varying degrees of success, but congregation B was built around the pulpit skills of its pastor and an exciting Sunday morning worship experience. It did not have the internal strength needed to weather the storms and prevent its collapse.

The Rest of the Story

Since congregation B's fourth pastor in five years came in 1993, they have been on a roller-coaster ride. Explosive growth built on the pastor's considerable pulpit skills and dynamic Sunday morning worship marked his first five years. This period of growth was followed by a period of painful contraction. At that time leadership determined it needed to address the instability and immaturity of the congregation.

Their strategy? Build a Sunday School.

Congregation A welcomed its fourth pastor in three years in 1991. He came believing that Sunday School and other ministries were out-of-date and determined to introduce a new ministry paradigm. Undervalued and neglected, the Sunday School immediately began to decline. In the pastor's first five years, Sunday School attendance dropped by more than 50 percent, and worship attendance declined each year. After nine years the Sunday School declined to about 300 and was then disbanded. Worship attendance continued to steadily decline, losing almost 50 percent since its peak and 33 percent since the new pastor came.

Both churches have stopped reporting Sunday School and worship attendance.

Lessons to Learn

Several lessons can be learned from these two churches.

1. Congregations built without the internal structures and strength that an effective Sunday School creates are more vulnerable and less likely to survive the storms of congregational life. *Big* doesn't equal *strong*.

2. Not all Sunday Schools are created equal. Saying a church has Sunday School isn't the same as saying a church has built a truly effective Sunday School ministry.

3. Developing and maintaining an effective Sunday School requires a consistent investment of time, effort, resources, and leadership.

4. Good Sunday Schools help the church reach and keep new people. Sunday School is an effective way to assimilate new people and retain growth.

5. Sunday Schools are fragile. What takes decades to build can be quickly destroyed by a lack of vision and neglect.

6. Relying heavily on a pastor's strengths is dangerous. Churches that develop a network of mature lay leaders through the Sunday School are stronger.

7. Through consistent discipling the Sunday School helps believers mature in their faith. Without individual maturity, congregational maturity is impossible.

8. Sunday Schools connect people and build love, loyalty, and unity in ways a morning worship experience can't.

9. A truly effective Sunday School cannot exist without the vision, leadership, and support of the pastor.

The Potential and Promise of the Sunday School

Congregations A and B illustrate patterns seen across the church world today. Many churches, like congregation A, are abandoning the Sunday School. They believe Sunday School is ineffective and outmoded and that a new era demands new ministry paradigms. In many cases the diagnosis is correct. But the cure is worse than the disease. Abandoning Sunday School all too often sacrifices ministry infrastructure essential for a healthy, growing church. In their search for something new, they replace the comprehensive, church-wide ministry of Sunday School with a patchwork of niche ministries. Often the church grows weaker rather than stronger.

Many other churches, like congregation B, grow rapidly but not well. Churches that fail to build ministry infrastructure to support morning worship attendance risk collapse. At best they embark on an attendance roller coaster. They never develop the stability and maturity needed to consolidate their gains and develop a pattern of healthy, consistent growth.

The ministry trajectories of both patterns ultimately intersect. Both end up without a cohesive ministry system. Morning worship is increasingly a gathering of strangers and decreasingly a gathering of brothers and sisters. Unity suffers. Spiritual growth suffers. Outreach and evangelism suffer. The church is less able to care, less able to assimilate newcomers, less able to impact the community, and less able to develop leaders.

The Last Word

Here's the bottom line: To fulfill God's purposes in the world, the church must reach the lost and help them become fully devoted disciples. It must help believers grow to spiritual maturity and give expression to their love of God in worship and in their daily lives. It must help create the bonds of love and loyalty among its members and bear witness to God's truth, in word and deed, in the world. Unfortunately, many churches are failing.

Of the ministries available to the church, Sunday School has the greatest potential to achieve these ends. Sunday School is the ideal tool. An outstanding infrastructure of curricula and training are already available. The church is demonstratively better able to fulfill God's purposes with a good Sunday School than without it. Finally, the church needs quality Sunday Schools today more than ever. Too many congregations are adrift with no vision or strategy. But there is an answer. We must trust God to give us the vision and use Sunday School as our strategy.

Now is the time to wake the sleeping giant.

Endnotes

[1] *World Book Encyclopedia*, 1957 ed., s.v. "Lincoln, Abraham."

[2] William J. Bennett, *The Book of Virtues* (New York: Simon and Schuster Publishing Company, 1993), 258.

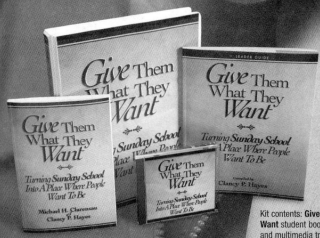

Change Lives
through Effective Teaching

Effective, equipped teachers will make a lasting impact on the lives of their students. **Make a Difference! Be a Teacher** training resources show teachers how to increase their effectiveness through the right attitudes and actions as well as explain the key elements that help students apply the Bible to their daily lives.

Leader Kit	**02JZ2004**
Student Book	**02JZ2005**
Spanish Student Book	**02JZ2006**

Kit contents: **Make a Difference! Be a Teacher** student book, leader guide, and multimedia training CD with English and Spanish PowerPoint® presentations and Spanish leader guide.

Call or check our Web site for current pricing.